Out Of Yamacraw And Beyond
Discovering Black Savannah

Charles Lwanga Hoskins

Copyright © 2002 by Charles Lwanga Hoskins

All rights reserved. No part of this book may be reproduced in any form or by any electronic or mechanical means including information storage and retrieval systems-except in the case of brief quotations embodied in critical articles or reviews-without permission in writing from its publisher, The Gullah Press.

First Printing, November 2002

ISBN: 0-9708215-1-4

Published by The Gullah Press

P.O. Box 994, Savannah, Georgia 31402

Funding for this publication provided by

The City of Savannah's

Department of Cultural Affairs/

Leisure Services Bureau's

**To
Westley Wallace Law
Freedom Fighter**

(Courtesy of the *Savannah Morning News*)

"Every shut eye ain' sleep and every goodbye ain' gone"

Table Of Contents

1. Acknowledgements
2. Introduction   11
3. Discovering Black Savannah   19
4. Images of the Black Experience   63
5. A Brief Chronology of Black Savannah   107
6. Index   139

Acknowledgements

Around 1978, the late Westley Wallace Law, that drum-major for African American history in Savannah, began a regularly scheduled tour of black Savannah. The endeavor was essentially to remind some and inform others, especially visitors to our fair city, of the remarkable heritage of the black experience in Savannah. The City Council's recent decision to construct a base for the African American Monument on River Street, and the monument itself, attest to the heightened awareness of the many contributions of African Americans to the advancement of Savannah. But black history has often suffered from a serious handicap. In 1952, Editor Sol C. Johnson of the *Savannah Tribune* lamented:

> In the absence of any media for preserving the memory of Negroes who have made worthwhile contributions to the life of our community, it is not strange that many of our citizens are ignorant of the fact that such individuals ever lived. It is a dishonor in part and in part ingratitude on the part of somebody that persons who spent much of their lives working, without thought of compensation, to promote the welfare of people, should be forgotten so soon and so permanently.

I hope that this work, which leans very heavily on the files of the *Savannah Tribune,* the *Savannah Morning News*, and publications of the City of Savannah, will help to fill this void in our memories, both for our generation and those yet to come. African Americans have been in Savannah from the beginning, as sawyers on loan from South Carolinians; hence, the black community here is the oldest in the state of Georgia. This book records some missing pages of Savannah's history. It is not a detailed study of black Savannah, but a reference guide which gives a limited over view of the 269 year odyssey of African Americans in Savannah. Throughout the period African Americans in Savannah have been called, and have called themselves, blacks, Negroes, or coloreds.

They have lived in several parts of this metropolis such as Arkwright Village, Little Tybee, Pin Point, Montgomery, Coffee Bluff, Grimball's Point, Rossingnol Hill, Woodville, Brownville, Dittermusville, Tatemville, Springfield, White Bluff, Dixon Park, the Victorian District, Bingville, Ogeecheeton, Tremont Park, Mexico City, Sandfly, Liberty City, and Cloverdale, to mention only a few.

Jefferson Hall contributed data for this study. Tania June Sammons graciously provided some editing and copy reading assistance and Judith W. Edwin helped with the layout of the book. I thank the City of Savannah's Department of Cultural Affairs/Leisure Services Bureau for their assistance with this publication. Finally I thank my wife Evalena, for her constant encouragement while this work was in progress. I lay sole claim to all the mistakes.

Charles Lwanga Hoskins

Introduction: African Americans in Savannah

The black presence in the Savannah area began with the arrival of Spaniards and Africans in 1526, around what is now called Sapelo Sound. Local African Americans tell a story that a ship of black men from Santo Domingo came up the Savannah River and conquered Spaniards on the coast long before James Edward Oglethorpe founded Georgia. At Oglethorpe's arrival a few South Carolinians loaned the Georgia colonists several slaves to assist in laying out the new settlement. Three slaves escaped on their way to Savannah. As Oglethorpe wrote, "I sent away the Negroes who sawed for us, for so long as they continued here our men were encouraged in idleness by their working for them." Two slaves were jailed for attacking their owner. Even though the Trustees banned slavery in the colony in 1735, Oglethorpe used 200 slaves to build a fort on St. Simon's Island. In 1740, many escaped slaves from South Carolina and Georgia fought with the Spaniards against Oglethorpe for the possession of Fort Mose in Florida. Meanwhile the colonists were said to have gone "stark mad after Negroes."

By 1750, slavery was allowed in Georgia. The comprehensive slave code of 1755, copied from the South Carolina code, contained stipulations which guaranteed white supremacy. It stated simply that slaves were to be kept at all times under "due order and subjection." Slaves were not allowed to keep drums or loud instruments, buy, sell or trade, raise horses or cattle without a license and not more than seven of them could gather together by themselves. They could hire out their time only with the permission of their owners. The first slaves came mainly from South Carolina and the West Indies. The first ship to bring slaves directly from Africa arrived in Savannah in 1766. African Americans smarted under the yoke of servitude, for to be a slave in Savannah was to live constantly under the possibility of violence and always subject to the whim of one's owner. A few incidents of resistance occurred; for example, in 1765 some fugitives established a camp on the Savannah River, but no general revolt was attempted. Blacks never had the urge to commit mass suicide.

As the American Revolution reached Savannah, the British governor 'impressed' 400 slaves to work on the fortifications of the town and armed an additional 200. A local black, Quamino Dolly, the patriarch of a well-known black family that owned property in the Trustees Garden, showed the British a safe path through the swamps, enabling them to surprise the American side. In 1779, about 500 to 800 blacks from Haiti arrived with the French fleet to aid the American forces. This group, sometimes called the Fontages, was established in 1716, and had as its motto "to die rather than fail." Among them was teenager Henri Christophe, who later led the only successful slave revolt in the Americas.

When the British left Savannah in July 1782, they took about thirty-five hundred blacks with them, including the Rev. George Liele who later founded the Baptist denomination in Jamaica. Perhaps the experience of soldiering influenced some blacks. About 300 armed blacks, calling themselves "King of England Soldiers," camped at Bear Creek and terrorized plantations on the Savannah River. The Georgia militia took about four years to subdue them. Slaves at Whitefield's Bethesda orphan home armed themselves and refused to surrender their freedom. Black defiance occurred again in 1791 and 1792.

From the beginning Savannah depended heavily on slave labor. The price of slaves tripled

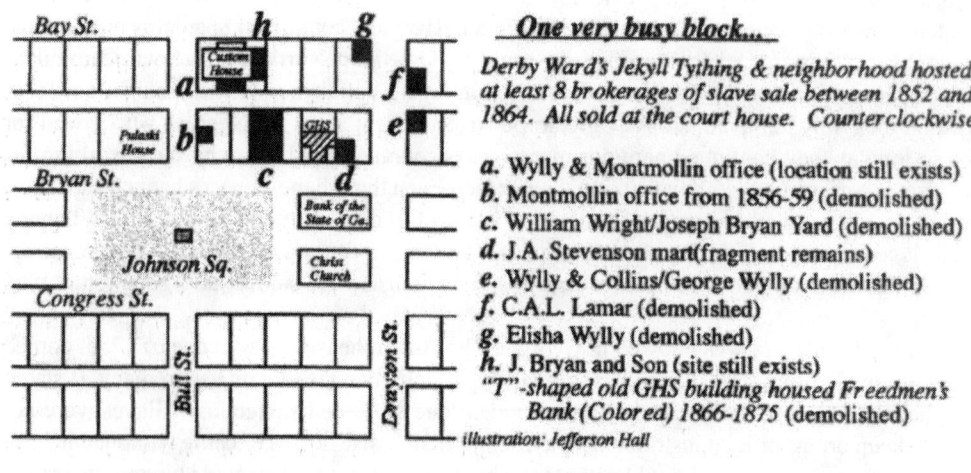

One very busy block...

Derby Ward's Jekyll Tything & neighborhood hosted at least 8 brokerages of slave sale between 1852 and 1864. All sold at the court house. Counterclockwise.

a. Wylly & Montmollin office (location still exists)
b. Montmollin office from 1856-59 (demolished)
c. William Wright/Joseph Bryan Yard (demolished)
d. J.A. Stevenson mart (fragment remains)
e. Wylly & Collins/George Wylly (demolished)
f. C.A.L. Lamar (demolished)
g. Elisha Wylly (demolished)
h. J. Bryan and Son (site still exists)
"T"-shaped old GHS building housed Freedmen's Bank (Colored) 1866-1875 (demolished)

illustration: Jefferson Hall

From Slave House to School House...

Decker Ward's Trust Lot "I" superstructure is comprised of three connected buildings, two of which were built as slave brokerages. At 19 & 21 Barnard St. both stand in tact, side by side at the entrance of today's City Market. No.19 (a) was built in 1855 for David R. Dillon, while tax digests indicate that No. 21 (b) was completed the next year for John Montmollin. After eight years as a slave brokerage the Montmollin property became the Savannah Educational Association's first school in early 1865. The Bryan Free School had 450 students. The principal was James Porter, a black man who before the war had operated an underground school within his adjacent tailoring business (c). He was later principal of the West Broad Street School and took a seat in Georgia's State Legislature.

illustration: Jefferson Hall

between 1800 and 1860. Rice production around the area was done by slaves, and slave labor made Savannah the lumber center on the Atlantic coast. Henry McAlpin and some 400 of his slaves at Hermitage plantation, made the famous Savannah gray bricks, operated an iron foundry, produced lumber, cultivated rice, and reared horses. The slaves lived in brick houses and had a hospital on the plantation.

Around 1821, several hundred slaves and free blacks were organized into fire companies. Some 500 slaves cleared the forest and laid the Central of Georgia rail line from Savannah to Macon. In time black hands in the interior of the state planted and picked the white cotton and other black hands transported the product from the storage depot to the ships, as Savannah became the leading cotton port in the Southeast. From about 1820, the call of Mother Africa exerted some influence over local blacks. In 1849, for example, approximately 181 people left Savannah. Choirs, and an immense crowd bid them goodbye. Among them was the Rev. Isaac Roberts, aged forty-seven, who was the pastor of the Third African Baptist Church and a "race man" in the terminology of that day, who had vocally expressed his disgust with slavery. The city fathers imposed a tax of two hundred dollars on any black leaving the town for Liberia. It was rumoured that some three hundred runaway slaves had gathered in Savannah to go to Liberia. On May 25, 1855, a letter in the *Daily Morning News* suggested that the Rev. Andrew Marshall be sent to the North on a "missionary journey" to enlighten Northerners about slavery, but no action was ever taken.

In March 1859, Joseph Bryan, one of Savannah's leading slavers, offered for sale the four hundred and thirty-six slaves on the Butler plantation located south of Savannah. This sale took place at the Tenbroeck race track some three miles from Savannah. The slaves, all full-blooded Africans, were housed in the stables. None had been previously sold. One reporter commented that some slaves showed "heavy grief" in their faces. The sale netted $303,850.

Savannah had the largest number of free blacks in the state. They first appeared in Colonial times. By 1793, following the defeat of the French in Haiti, several white and black families left the island for Savannah. In 1840, Savannah was home to 632 free blacks. The number grew to 686 in 1850, and to seven hundred and five in 1860. A law passed in 1810 compelled all free blacks entering the state to register. They had to buy a ten dollar badge to work, pay fifty cents each year to register with the clerk of Inferior Court, and have a white guardian. Several free people of color owned slaves. In 1823, the number peaked with some fifty-eight slaves owned by colored people. Years later they also had to perform public work for the city. By 1850, some seventy percent of Savannah's free people of color were mulattos. A few free African Americans enjoyed privileges above their station.

Father Andrew C. Marshall, born in South Carolina, came to Savannah in 1766. He bought his freedom and became rather wealthy through his drayage business, employing mainly free labor. He succeeded his uncle, the sainted Father Andrew Bryan, as pastor of the Colored Baptist Church, serving in that capacity for over forty years. In the 1850s, he owned several pieces of property, four carriages, and stocks and bonds in the Marine and Fire Insurance Bank, for a total of nearly $40,000. Another mulatto, Anthony Odingsells, inherited his property from his white father. In the 1820s he owned fifteen slaves and two hundred acres. He was a gentleman farmer and fisherman.

Tailors from Haiti were also among the few prosperous blacks. Louis Mirault made suits for some of the city's leading white citizens. When he died in 1828 he owned six slaves and had real property worth one thousand dollars. William Claghorn, founder of St. Stephen's Episcopal Church, later called St. Matthew's Episcopal Church, was a baker and caterer whose clientele included some of the richest people in Savannah. He employed two German bakers. In 1860, he had property valued at $4,500 as well as $2,000 in personal property. That year free African Americans owned property valued at sixty-one thousand dollars.

Among the women, pastry workers and seamstresses enjoyed a brisk trade. Aspasia Mirault operated a confectionery at Bull and Broughton Streets and another at Broughton and Whitaker Streets. Mary Woodhouse and Matilda Taylor ran underground schools. West Indian born Catherine Deveaux, a seamstress, and her daughter, Jane, also ran an underground school for almost thirty years. The Rev. John B. Deveaux sent his daughter to his sister in Albany, New York, for her education. When General Sherman entered Savannah, Miss Deveaux was still teaching her fellow blacks. Julien Fromantin, a Haitian, was the first black to operate an underground school. James Porter, Louis B. Toomer, and James M. Simms also operated underground schools. Simms, whose school was on Berrien Street, is the only black Savannahian known to have been publicly whipped for teaching blacks to read and write. In 1865, Simms called for the election or appointment of local black policemen, congressmen and other officials.

In June 1861, several free colored women offered their services to General A. R. Lawton to sew one hundred suits for the Confederate soldiers. Sixty free black men also offered to serve in the army in any capacity. Some had worked on the fortifications at Fort Pulaski and were thanked for their efforts. In May, one free black and one slave donated ten dollars each to the South's "cause." In September, 160 slaves began to construct a battery below Fort Jackson. They were reported to have worked "well and cheerfully singing over their hoes and axes." General Mercer received authority from the Secretary of War to 'impress' Negroes sufficient to construct fortifications necessary for the defense of Savannah. In all, some 2,500 slaves worked on the fortifications to defend Savannah. In 1862, the city authorities allowed some blacks to sponsor a ball with the proceeds going towards the sick and wounded Confederate soldiers.

Black Frank, a slave, and his owner George W. Stiles, were born around the same time. They were inseparable as kids growing up. Frank played the bugle and George the piano. Both went off to the Civil War together in the Savannah Volunteer Guards, where Frank played his bugle. They returned to Savannah and continued to be inseparable. When George died he was buried in Laurel Grove Cemetery North. Eventually Frank also died and he was buried in Laurel Grove Cemetery South, and it may be, as the Negro spiritual has it, "their eyes are watching God" for an explanation of the separation. Dick Footman also went off to war with his owner Neal Habersham but never returned to the city. John H. Deveaux served with the Confederate Mosquito Fleet.

Joe Parkman, "ole Joe," was a slave fifer who went away with his company. He accidentally drank poison and died near the Appomattox Court House. He was buried "with full military honors" in an unmarked grave in Virginia. William Waters, born in 1832, was a drum sergeant with the Republican Blues, Louis Du Bross, a fifer, Joe Verdery and Jack Bolton, kettle drummers and Dave Ellison a bass drummer served with the Savannah Volunteer Guards. Their skills were said to have been "extraordinary." They were but the latest version of "Boy Chatham," a slave bugler owned by a white syndicate in 1809.

On Thursday, January 12, 1865, General William T. Sherman and Secretary of War Edwin M. Stanton met with twenty black leaders at Sherman's headquarters. The Rev. Garrison Frazier, the group's leader, was asked to define the experience of slavery. He stated that slavery was "receiving by irresistible force the work of another man and not by his consent." Freedom he defined as "taking us from under the yoke of bondage and placing us where we could reap the fruit of our labor, take care of ourselves and assist the government in maintaining our freedom."

During the short post-war respite, James Porter and James Simms won election to the Georgia House, as blacks voted for the first time. Richard White won the election for clerk of the Superior Court and Albert Jackson was one of the commissioners of registration. The Governor appointed James M. Simms judge of a District Court but he never occupied the position. In 1898, President William McKinley appointed John H. Deveaux head of customs in Savannah. He kept that position until his death in 1909. The English have a saying, as their monarchs succeed one another "The King is dead; long live the King." In the twinkling of an eye, the old white obsession to keep blacks "under due order and subjection" re-asserted itself. All the black legislators were expelled and by the early 1900's Jim Crow was King. The "two Savannahs" policy became the cardinal article of faith and it was rigidly enforced, and a long, long period of agony followed.

Blacks had to fall back on their own resources. By 1914, black Savannah had two banks, one theater, one drug store and one dry goods store. Three funeral establishments did a brisk business supported by five insurance companies providing sick and death benefits. Several small grocery shops flourished as well as ice cream parlors. Savannah had fourteen physicians, three dentists, four lawyers, one photographer and three real estate agents. A branch of the National Negro Business League, an employment agency, and business school in the parish hall of St. Augustine's Episcopal Church, contributed to the advancement of black Savannah. In addition, blacks had over three hundred lodges and societies. Furthermore, there were ninety-three churches or one church for every three hundred and fifty-seven blacks.

In 1917, James Weldon Johnson established a local branch of the NAACP with Dr. Fanon S. Belcher as president and attorney James G. Lemon as secretary. The branch held a membership drive in 1918. Annual membership cost one dollar. The principal concerns of the group centered on the treatment of blacks on street cars, in public places, and in the police courts. The branch also opposed placing houses of prostitution in black areas. In 1930, the *Savannah Tribune* reported the formation of another NAACP local chapter at McKelvey-Powell auditorium. Donald Thomas, a glazier, was elected president, N. A. Branham was vice-president, Samuel A. Brown, secretary, and the Rev. John Q. Adams was treasurer. An executive board of twenty-five persons was also elected.

It was not until the 1940s that some relief appeared on the horizon. The Rev. Ralph Mark Gilbert, pastor of First African Baptist Church, and others, registered some nineteen thousand blacks which gave the group the leverage to pressure Mayor John Kennedy to appoint nine black policemen, nearly one hundred years after James M. Simms had asked for them. The reinvigorated NAACP was very effective in gaining political rights for blacks. In 1968, Bobby Hill became the first black elected to the Georgia House of Representatives since reconstruction and the Rev. L. Scott Stell was the first black elected to the Chatham County Commission. Lawrence D. Perry and Mrs. Esther F. Garrison were appointed to the Board of Education. In 1970, Bowles C. Ford became the first black ever elected to the City Council. Nine years later, Governor George Busbee appointed attorney Eugene Gadsden a judge of the Superior Court. In 1995, Alderman Floyd Adams Jr. was elected mayor of Savannah.

American Missionary Association.
SCHOOLS FOR FREEDMEN.
TEACHER'S MONTHLY REPORT.

Name of Teacher, *Louis B. Toomer*
in the school called *Oglethorpe Primary School*
at *Savannah* County (or Parish) of *Chatham*
State of *Georgia* for Month of *November* 186*6*.

No. of days the school was kept during the calender month, _____ No. of hours each day, _____
If absent any number of days, how many? _____ Cause? _____
" " " hours, " " _____ Cause? _____
No. of different pupils, *127* New _____ No. transferred from other schools, _____ Average attendance, *80*
No. of males, _____ No. females, _____ No. adults (over 18), _____ No. white, _____
No. in Primary studies, _____ Intermediate, _____ Advanced, _____
No. who write, on slates only, _____ do. with pen, _____
Is Singing taught in school? _____ Calisthenics or Gymnastics? _____
No. sessions in Night school, _____ Name of the school, _____ Average attendance, _____
" " Sabbath schools, _____ " " _____ " " _____
Amount, if any, received for tuition, _____
No. of visits made in colored families, _____
No. of Bibles distributed, _____ No. of Testaments, _____
No. of Books, _____ Tracts and Papers, _____
No. of families in which you have engaged in religious services, either by reading the Scriptures, singing, or prayer, _____

No. of hopeful conversions, if any, during the month, _____

Items for Freedman's Bureau, not given above:
No. in Alphabet, _____ Who spell and read bf easy lessons, _____ In advanced readers, _____
In Geography, _____ in Arithmetic, _____ in higher branches, _____
No. free before the War, _____

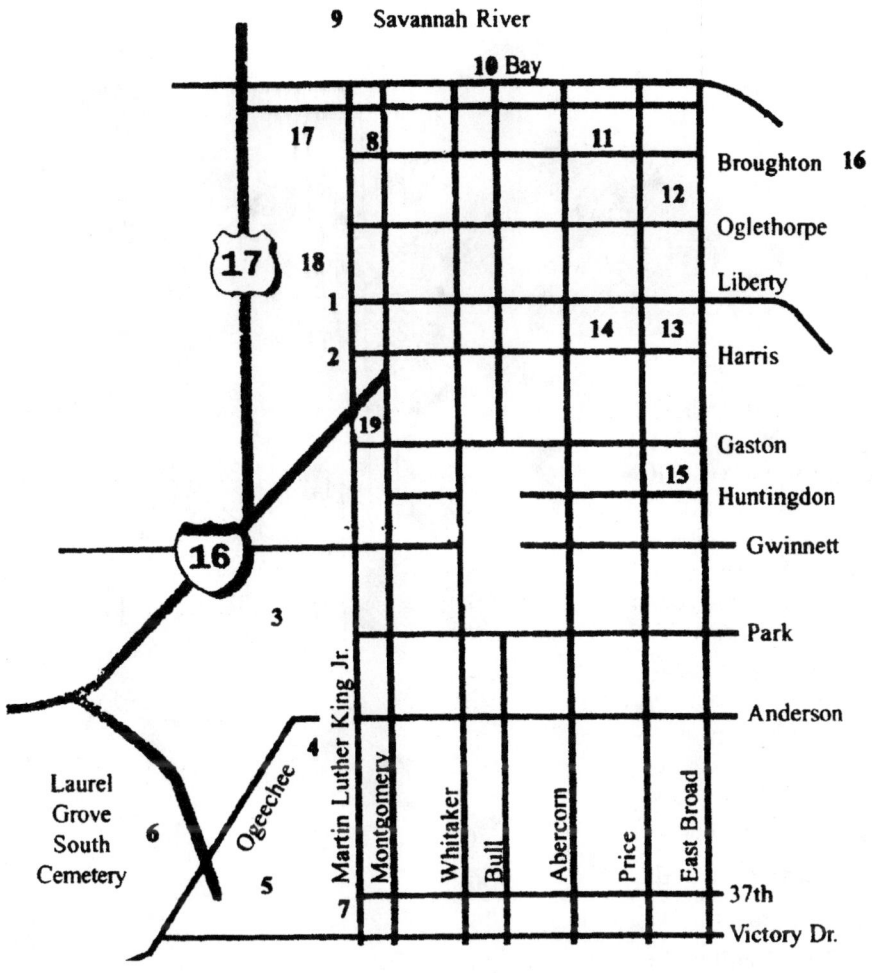

(Courtesy of the *Savannah Morning News*)

Legend

1. Visitor Center. 2. Frog Town. 3. CurryTown/Bethlehem Missionary Baptist Church. 4. St. Matthew's Episcopal Church. 5. Cuyler/Brownville. 6. Laurel Grove South Cemetery. 7. Martin Luther King Jr. Blvd. 8. Franklin Square/First African Baptist Church. 9. Savannah River/River Street. 10. Bay Street. 11. Underground School. 12. Greene Square/Second African Baptist Church. 13. Beach Institute/Beach Neighborhood. 14. Troup Square/Unitarian/St. Stephen's Episcopal Church. 15. King-Tisdell Cottage. 16. Broughton Street. 17. Yamacraw/First Bryan Baptist Church. 18. Turner Blvd./St. Phillip's A.M.E. 19. Ralph Mark Gilbert Civil Rights Museum.

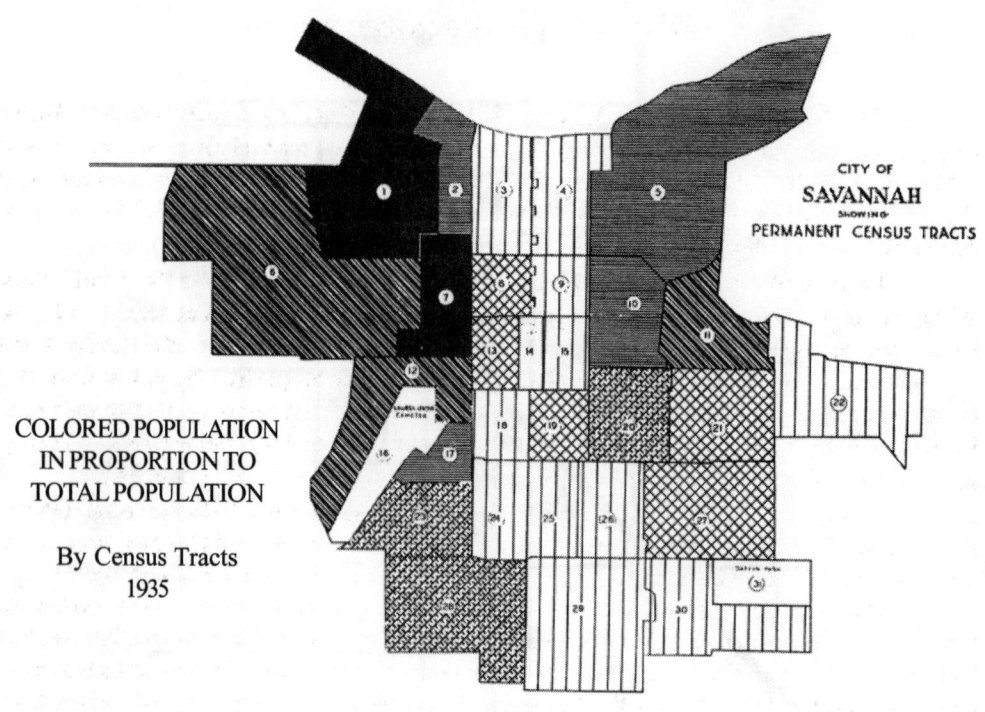

18

Discovering Black Savannah

The Savannah Visitor Center, 301 Martin Luther King Boulevard, was the Central of Georgia railroad station. The railroad was one of the largest commercial slave owners in Savannah with 126 slaves. In 1820, over fifty percent of households in Savannah owned slaves and in 1860, about thirty-three percent owned slaves. Draymen, poor Irish, free coloreds, and slaves, transported cotton from the warehouse to the ships on the river.

Frog Town is located on the northwestern section of Savannah from the end of Yamacraw at Hull Street on Martin L. King Jr., Boulevard to around Gwinnett Street. The area probably got its name from the frog population in the swamps off West Boundary Street. Even after slavery, hundreds of blacks continued to work for Central of Georgia. Many Gullah people from South Carolina, lived on the dirt streets among the tracks and offices of the railroad in a "hodge-podge of unpainted houses." In addition to their lack of paint, many houses had no indoor plumbing. Some Greeks, German and Polish Jews, and other ethnic merchants owned "plenty of grocery stores" in the area.

Albert Kemp, a blackman, came from Ludowici to Savannah in 1918 and rented a store near the corner of Cohen and Guerard Streets. Around 1943, he bought a lot, built his own store, a market, a recreation hall, and a beauty parlor near the store. His family lived on the second floor.

Union Branch Baptist Church, St. Luke's Baptist, and Metropolitan Baptist, were scattered throughout Frog Town. Milton Hall, one of the original nine black policemen, and Savannah's first black motorcycle policeman, with his stunts made famous later by Evel Knievel, was a feature of the area. Hall was regarded as "the South's best known Negro motorcycle race rider," and had membership in the American Motorcycle Association in the class B group. Hall died in a motorcycle accident in Langhorne, Pennsylvania, in 1956. When Savannah was a "swinging town," Frog Town was noted for its moonshine stills and bordellos. Frog Town was completely destroyed by urban renewal.

The Springhill Redoubt, where the Siege of Savannah occurred, is Frog Town's other claim to fame. There, in October 1779, some 800 black Haitians fought on the side of the Americans, while 200 local armed blacks fought on the side of the British. Two Jewish cemeteries, the third oldest in the country, on Cohen Street, dating from the 1770s, grace the area. The old Union Station and repair yards of Central of Georgia are also located there. Esther Garrison Elementary School on Berrien Street now honors the first black woman to sit on the Board of Education.

Curry Town is located west of Martin L. King Jr., Boulevard, where Frazier homes now stand. The Masonic Temple was located near Connors Temple Church, and the area had many businesses, clubs and residences.

Robert W. Gadsden School. Prof. Robert W. Gadsden was born in Sandersville, Georgia, in 1874, and some years later moved with his family to Savannah. He attended West Broad Street School (the William Scarbrough House, now the Ships of the Sea Museum) under Principal James H. C. Butler. In his eighty-seven page autobiography Gadsden wrote:

> I wanted very much to go to Atlanta University because I knew most of my elementary teachers went there. I knew that Albert Ashton, John Taylor, James

First Church/Old Jerusalem
(Courtesy the *Savannah Tribune*)

The Rev. George Liele

The Rev. Andrew Bryan

Coffee and Alonzo Baker went there, too, but I did not dream that I would ever get there. And I cannot express the feeling that came over me when my mother informed me that I was to go there also.

Gadsden graduated from Atlanta University, returned to Savannah, and began teaching at East Broad Street School in 1902. Two years later he was appointed principal of the school. He served as principal of two schools for many years. He retired in 1947 after forty-five years with the system. An editorial in the *Savannah Tribune* stated that Prof. Gadsden was "doing much to put the stamp of worth upon our children."

Prof. Gadsden was married to teachers Laura Louise Hutchinson and then to Geneva L. Stiles. His two daughters, Lucy Gadsden Solomon and Margie Gadsden Caution, and granddaughters Laura Solomon Vault and Margaret Solomon Brown also became teachers. This one family taught school in Savannah for a total of 170 years. All triggered by a mother, Lucy Noble Gadsden, who was a washer woman suffering from asthma, who had only a third grade education and could not correct her son's eighth grade homework, but she could surely "check" him. In 1955, the Board of Education named the Curry Town School in Prof. Gadsden's honor.

Canaan Land. The Rev. George Liele began preaching the gospel along the Savannah River sometime in the 1770s, and baptized Andrew Bryan. In January 1788, the Rev. Abraham Marshall, a white man, and the Rev. Jesse Peter, a black man, ordained Andrew Bryan and installed him as the first pastor of the Ethiopian Church of Jesus Christ in Savannah. Our elders called this original congregation Old Jerusalem. On this foundation we can say that the First African Baptist Church, First Bryan Baptist Church, Second African Baptist Church, St. Matthew's Episcopal Church and Bethlehem Baptist Church, all founded by blacks during slavery, are the elder daughters of Old Jerusalem.

David Margate, a black Anglican deacon, began his ministry at the Rev. George Whitefield's Bethesda orphan home, near Savannah, around the same time as George Liele. He preached a sermon at Bethesda claiming that God had appointed him as the Moses, to lead the slaves to freedom. Within weeks he found himself on a boat headed for England. The Rev. George Liele left with the British in 1782, and went to Jamaica where he established the Baptist denomination. The Rev. David George also left Savannah and went to Nova Scotia, Canada, and then, to Sierra Leone in Africa. He established Baptist churches in both places.

Bethlehem Missionary Baptist Church was organized February 5, 1859, when the Rev. Isaac Brown, Jerry Burke, Frank Lloyd, and Eli Brown received letters of transfer from First African Baptist Church summoning them to form a new congregation. This new congregation met in Stoval Hall on Liberty Street. The congregation later bought a lot on Price Street under the leadership of their second pastor, the Rev. Edward Brown, and constructed their first building in 1873. Several short pastorates followed.

The Rev. David Canty, a "son" of Bethlehem Baptist Church, became pastor in 1924 and served for fifteen years. As a member he had held almost every office in the church. In 1913, he was ordained a deacon and ten years later was ordained a minister. Canty was also superintendent at Pilgrim Insurance Company. The Rev. David Canty started a building fund at Bethlehem, but the

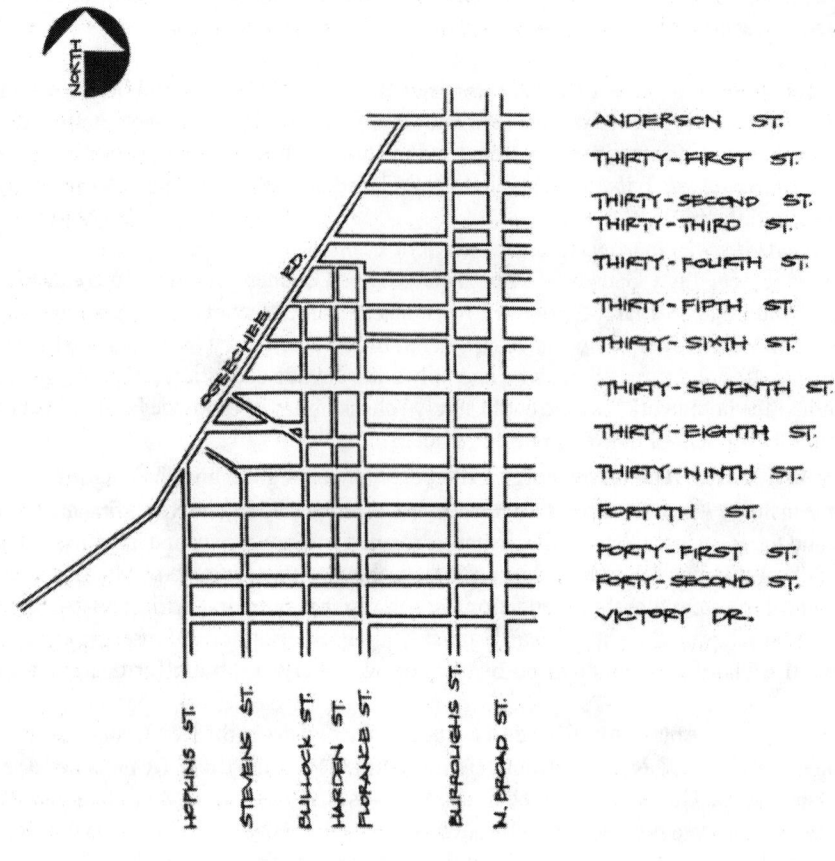

(Courtesy The City of Savannah)

Depression killed those dreams. He improved the physical appearance of the church, installed a baptismal pool and organized several new ministries. In 1930, the church was located at Park Avenue and Cuyler Street. The Rev. Sherman A. Baker served for nineteen years. During his pastorate, a new church was built in 1946.

The Rev. Louis Scott Stell, Jr., was installed as pastor of Bethlehem Missionary Baptist Church on March 31, 1952. His arrival was the harbinger of a new phase in the church's life. Stell served for thirty-three years, the longest pastorate in the church's history. The interior of the church was renovated, central heating and new stained glass windows were installed, the sanctuary was carpeted and padded pews were added along with a new public address system. Bethlehem was the first black church to install a glass baptismal pool.

Stell, a social activist, served as education committee chair of the NAACP for many years and in 1962 joined thirty-seven other persons to sue the Board of Education over school segregation. He was the first black elected a Chatham County Commissioner in 1968. He ordained or licensed over twenty-six ministers, and deacons, including two of his sons, the Rev. Larry Stell, pastor of Central Baptist Church and the Rev. Louis S. Stell. The Chatham County Commissioners named a one hundred acre park in his honor.

Cuyler/Brownville. Dr. Louis A. Falligant owned a nineteen and a half acre tract of land south of the city called Brownville or Brownsville, in 1867. It spanned Florence, Bulloch, Thirty-six and Forty-Second Street. David R. Dillon bought a one hundred acre tract on the east side of Brownville. African Americans flocked to Savannah immediately after the Civil War and settled on the fringes of the city. In September 1883, the Legislature authorized the extension of the city limits to Forty-Second Street, (then Twelfth Street) and the city improved the property. Many homes were built for blacks in the northern section of the area between the 1880s and 1930s. The earliest houses, known as Meldrim row, were built on west Thirty-Third and Thirty-Fourth Streets. By 1900, the population of the area was majority black. The present Cuyler/Brownville area is bounded by Laurel Grove Cemetery South, Anderson Street, Martin L. King, Jr., Boulevard, and West Victory Drive.

The late John Lyons remembered the Cuyler/Brownville area as an "exclusive neighborhood," inhabited by the black bourgeoisie who were "about to leave their mark on Savannah." Newspaper owner Floyd Adams, Sr., banker Louis B. Toomer, the Rev. Ralph Mark Gilbert, pastor of the First African Baptist Church and president of the local branch of the NAACP, Principal Robert Gadsden, funeral director Sidney Jones, Dr. J. W. Jamerson, Jr., real estate agent D. J. Hill, Donald Thomas, a glazier, and many others anchored this black enclave. The civil rights successes of the 1960s helped to make the area a less desirable locality for the black middle class and they soon abandoned the neighborhood. In 1996, it was reported that the neighborhood had a home ownership of twenty-nine percent, while the city as a whole had an ownership rate of fifty-one percent.

Cuyler Street School. In 1913, the Board of Education built a manual training shop, costing twenty-five hundred dollars, on the grounds of the old Haven Home School, which the Methodist Church opened in 1885. The following year the Board built the first public school for blacks, Cuyler Street School at the corner of Cuyler and Anderson Streets. This twenty-one room, two story masonry building with a basement, constructed in the Colonial Revival style, cost $52,500 and was built on a lot that measured two hundred and thirty feet by three hundred feet. Over time it housed

Charity Hospital
(Courtesy *The Savannah Tribune*)

St. Matthew's Episcopal Church
(Courtesy St. Matthew's Collection)

junior and senior high schools. All previous black schools had been converted churches or halls. The school at one time housed twelve hundred students. Split sessions were the order of the day as there was hardly adequate classroom space for blacks. John W. Hubert was the first principal. When the elementary division was moved to Florence Street School, Beach Senior High moved into the Cuyler Street School building and Hubert became principal of the junior and senior high schools. Some blacks wanted the combined school to be called Cuyler Senior High School. The School Superintendent informed the *Savannah Tribune* that the name Beach would not be dropped from the school. An annex was added in the 1930s. The Board built Beach High School on Hopkins Street in 1950. Cuyler Street School closed in 1975.

St. Stephen's/St. Matthew's, now at 1401 Martin L. King Jr. Boulevard, was organized in the winter of 1855 by a group of nine free coloreds in William Claghorn's bakery at the corner of Perry Lane and Habersham Street. West Indian born, the Rev. J. Robert Love, rector of St. Stephen's Episcopal Church, left the church in 1872, and founded St. Augustine's Episcopal Church in Yamacraw. In 1892, another West Indian, the Rev. Richard Bright, the first black Episcopal priest ordained in Georgia, became rector and soon opened a kindergarten and elementary school. He abolished pew rents, and published a catechism for the Sunday school. St. Stephen's congregation remained at Troup Square until 1943 when it merged with St. Augustine's Episcopal Church on West Broad Street and changed its name to St. Matthew's Episcopal Church.

John C. LeBey designed the Greek revival style church with four Doric columns and the Karl Kemp Construction Company was the builder. Major Thomas J. Hopkins was the electrical contractor. The new church was completed in 1948 at the cost of about $75,000. Father Gustave H. Caution, rector of St. Stephen's from 1931 to 1938, became rector of the congregation at its new location, and the church registered a large increase in membership. Father Harry Nevels was the first "son" of the church to serve as rector. In the 1970s, he started a kindergarten in the parish hall that is still in existence.

Trinidad born, Father Charles L. Hoskins, became rector of the congregation in 1975. During his administration, thirteen stained glass windows, that memorialized black parishes in Georgia, were installed in the 1980s, and the entire edifice was upgraded. In 1992, the congregation added the $315,000 dollar Toomer/Walker Social Hall. A history of the church was published in 1995. The marble baptismal font in the narthex has been used by the church for more than one hundred years.

McKane Hospital and Training School for Nurses/CharityHospital. In September1893, Dr. Alice Woodby McKane, the first black female doctor to practice in Savannah, established the McKane Training School for Nurses on the Northwest corner of Montgomery and Liberty Streets. The McKanes left Savannah for Liberia after their first class of nurses graduated in 1895. Several months later they returned to Savannah, and moved the training school to Florence and Sixth Street, now Thirty-Six Street, and added a hospital component for women and children. The hospital was incorporated June 1, 1896. The South Atlantic Medical Society, a group comprised of all the black doctors and druggists in the city, founded in 1892, assisted the work of the Hospital.

The *Savannah Tribune* noted the importance of the hospital for black folks. The hospital was organized and managed "by their own people irrespective of creed," and it afforded "relief to many a poor suffering woman and child who without its shelter and treatment might meet a miserable and untimely death." And, finally, because "it opens up an avenue of respectable livelihood and usefulness to our young women who have heretofore been limited to the cook pot, the school room, the wash tub or sewing machine."

By 1901, the McKanes, strong proponents of black self help and independence, severed their relationship with the hospital because most of the trustees wanted to accept grants from the city. The name was changed to Charity Hospital and Training School for Nurses. Later, in 1926, ground was broken for a new hospital at 644 West Thirty-Six Street. Many white citizens joined the effort and Mrs. Henry W. Mills Hodge and the Rosenwald Fund contributed heavily to the project. Cletus W. Bergen built the Colonial revival style hospital in 1931 for $125,000. Two years later, the Hospital served 2,009 patients with 334 paying their way. The State Board of Nurse Examiners closed the nursing school in 1938.

In 1940, a tablet in honor of Mrs. Lucy Lucas was placed in the main lobby of the hospital. Lucas was born in Savannah July 1, 1856, at 1245 Abercorn Street, and spent most of her life in the city. She had labored tirelessly for many years to advance the work of the institution and the construction of the new hospital. At her death in 1951, *Savannah Tribune* editor Sol Johnson remarked that she will be remembered by "Savannahians, white and colored, as one of the city's most useful citizens." The hospital added a psychiatric ward in memory of G. K. Gannam. Charity Hospital closed in 1964.

Within months, the William A. Harris Hospital and Nursing Home, a black private facility, opened in the building. The facility closed in 1976. Over the years a neighborhood group saved the institution from demolition and gained possession of the building. A fire in 1983, damaged the second floor and roof of the building and the Georgia Federal Savings and Loan deeded the property to the Cuyler community organization for $5,000. A second fire damaged the first floor and ceiling of the facility. The building was placed on the National Register of Historic places in 1985. Four years later the Cuyler Community Improvement Association failed in its attempt to obtain funds from the Department of Housing and Urban Development to rehabilitate the hospital.

In 1995, the city agreed to lend Tidelands Mental Retardation and Substance Abuse Center $400,000 to renovate the property for "the working poor" and people with drug problems. Some two years later Tidelands transferred the venture to Mercy Housing Southeast. As of this writing, Mercy Housing Southeast is spending nearly $8 million Federal dollars to develop eighty-eight units of affordable housing in the old hospital building and the former Florence Street School.

St. Mary's Catholic School. In 1907, Father Ignatius Lissner opened St. Mary's School at 902 West Thirty-Six Street, at Bulloch Street, for black students. The school was regarded as "a fitting monument to the other educational institutions which we are afforded by the Catholics and which are to be found in almost every section of our city." In 1917, Lissner also established the Franciscan Handmaids of the Most Pure Heart of Mary, an order of black nuns, who taught in the school. The two-story masonry building measuring forty-three by seventy-three feet was made of the "most durable pressed brick," and was in the Colonial Revival style. The school closed in 1977.

Florence Street School. The expansion of the black population in a southeasterly direction necessitated the erection of a new elementary school in that section. The Board of Education built its second school for blacks in 1929. Florence Street School was built on a lot approximately 200 x 240 feet for the sum of $9,494. The three-story masonry building cost $97,145 and faced West Thirty-Fifth Street, between Florence and Harden Streets. Miss Emma Quinney, who lived in the neighborhood, was appointed the first principal when the school opened February 10, 1930. Within a year, the twenty-one classrooms were in use. A Parent Teacher Association was organized in 1931.

Mills Memorial Home. Beginning in 1892, blacks had attempted to establish a home for the elderly community. Margaret Hall headed a group which bought several lots in East Savannah and operated a two-story facility which accommodated several persons. Hall's death ended this effort. In the 1920s, the Negro Women's Federation of Savannah spearheaded the erection of a home for poor blacks. The original idea was to locate the building in Thunderbolt, but at a public meeting Mrs. Sarah Hodge, a white woman, suggested that the home be placed on Ogeechee Road and that she would erect the building in memory of her parents, Mr. and Mrs. George Mills. The black community was required to raise enough funds to buy the land. Mrs. Hodge paid the $50,000 to erect the building and established a $150,000 endowment for its upkeep. The home, operated by an executive board of eighteen white women, and a black board of managers, opened November 22, 1925, at Ogeechee Road and Fortieth Street.

Superintendent Charlotte Spaulding Curley was in charge of the day-to-day running of the home. She was a trained social worker and previously worked for the Red Cross in Tuskegee, Alabama, for twelve years. Lucille Russell was the cook, Logan Russell, janitor, Lennie Burnett, nurse, and Bessie Davenport was the housekeeper. Occupants had to be at least sixty years old and have no living relative. The facility was described as "modern, well-equipped" with "all the conveniences of any well built home." Incorporated on June 9, 1925, the facility had twenty-five rooms and twenty-eight residents. The advent of old age assistance in 1937 necessitated a change in the by-laws to accept clients from the county welfare department. Twenty-three years later, the operators changed the facility into a nursing home.

Bishop Charles Manuel (Sweet Daddy) Grace established the House of Prayer at 643 Bismarck Street, later Thirty-First Street, in 1926. The Bishop conducted a religious revival in an openair tent at Thirty-Third and Burroughs Streets, where several people reported being cured of physical ailments. More than 5,000 people attended the twice-daily sessions. This religious endeavor; however, was immediately challenged. Elder J. W. Manns, president of the General Assembly of Free Seventh-Day Adventists, regarded the work of Bishop Grace and his associates as "a fake, it is a camouflage and all the rest of it." Not to be outdone, the Bishop reportedly stated that unless Manns recanted his charge the elder's jaw would be "locked."

Manns swore out a warrant on the Bishop, who was arrested as he entered his tent. However, the Bishop posted bond, returned to the revival and preached until "long after midnight." The Bishop attracted mostly formerly-rural people who had recently entered the city. The staid black Baptist congregations did not appreciate the Bishop's version of the gospel, particularly the high level of emotionalism and the style of music used in his service, especially brass instruments. Efforts by the Baptist establishment to stifle Bishop Grace came to naught.

In 1928, Bishop Grace led a procession "several city blocks long," from the House of Prayer at Bismarck Street to Ogeechee Road where 300 persons were baptized in an improvised pool. The congregation was reportedly "spreading rapidly in this section." In 1939, Bishop Grace complained that a woman in whose house he stayed while in the city had stolen $4,000 from him. The matter was settled in court.

Bishop Grace celebrated his twenty-first visit to Savannah in 1947. He began the day by baptizing 200 persons in a pool on Victory Drive. A procession that day was led by approximately one hundred youths on bicycles followed by "a colored city policeman who rode a motorcycle adorned with a dozen lights and fancy ornaments." The Bishop appeared "dressed in a robe of black trimmed in gold with his coat of arms on one sleeve." His hair and finger nails were long and he was flanked by "Grace Soldiers."

On his last visit to Savannah in 1959, the Bishop headed his annual parade in "his spectacular Cadillac," his long curly hair touching his shoulders. These parades had a positive cumulative effect on the music of black Savannah. The Bishop's visits were occasions for the faithful to bestow "a shower of cash gifts" on him. On entering the House of Prayer he approached the sawdust-filled altar as his followers thrilled by his presence, fell to the ground and danced and shrieked with joy. They never failed to put money in his hand first. At his death it was said that he had baptized more than 4,000 people in Savannah.

Palen United Methodist Church, formerly Palen Memorial Church, was built around 1920 at 1907 Burroughs Street. This masonry building was constructed in the Italianate style with a wood-framed tower and wide overhanging eaves and framed windows with arched brick crowns.

The Most Pure Heart of Mary, a one story wood-framed Catholic Church at 902 West Thirty-Sixth Street near Meldrim Row, was built around 1909. The church was brick veneered in the late 1970s. St. Mary's School at Thirty-Sixth and Burroughs Streets was run by the Franciscan sisters.

Laurel Grove Cemetery South on the western boundary of the Cuyler/Brownville neighborhood, off the Thirty-Seventh Street connector, was opened in 1852. Fifteen acres were set aside for the burial of "free persons of color and slaves." The first burial ground for people of color was "laid out and enclosed in a line with the (Colonial Park) cemetery," in 1763. According to Jefferson Hall, the burial ground probably "spanned a plot of ground from what is today the Rose of Sharon Apartments over toward the current Jones Street area. Its exact position and size remains to us imprecise at best, as it varies considerably from map to map." This cemetery was used until Laurel Grove South was opened. To this day, Laurel Grove Cemetery steadfastly maintains the "two Savannahs" prevalent at its founding, one white and the other black. By 1855, blacks who were buried in the black cemetery on the east side of Savannah near Whitefield Square were exhumed and re-interred in Laurel Grove South.

A *Savannah Morning News* reporter in 1888 observed that "the graves themselves bear the marks of frequent visits and flowers bloom on every hand." They were adorned with "shells, coral, vases, pitchers, goblets and glasses ... a washbowl and pitcher seem to be very popular with them." The tombstone shared by the Reverends Andrew Bryan, Henry Cunningham and Andrew Marshall is perhaps the most imposing of the lot. As the news reporter stated "the veneration of the churches for their pastors is more pronounced among colored people than among the whites."

Several slaves and free people of color who aided the Confederate cause are buried in Laurel Grove South. Old Tom, a slave of Captain John Wheaton, went off to war with his owner and returned to the city. At his burial in 1904, a Southern Cross was placed on his tomb. The Rev. Alexander Harris was born free to free parents in 1818. He served as a musician in the Confederate army. His funeral in 1909, was attended by several former Confederate soldiers. The Daughters of the Confederacy placed a Southern Cross on his tomb.

On the other side of the ledger, many blacks rendered invaluable service to the Union cause. After the Civil War, black Savannahians established a Col. Robert G. Shaw Veteran Post and the veterans participated in Decoration Day parades. Samuel Gordon Morse was the first Savannahian to enlist in the Union forces, followed by John Nesbitt and Edward Wicks. Wicks was born in Savannah in 1842, and served First Bryan Baptist Church as a deacon for fifty years. He was also the clerk of the church for thirty-four years. After the Civil War, he was Adjutant of the Robert Shaw Post of the Grand Army of the Republic. The Rev. James M. Simms is the only black we know of who was publicly whipped for teaching blacks to read and write. He helped establish the Republican Party and black Masons in Savannah. The Rev. Ulysses L. Houston led one thousand blacks to Skidaway Island following General Saxton's explanation of Sherman's Special Order # 15.

Laurel Grove Cemetery South is almost "holy ground," because it serves as the repository of the whole sweep of Savannah's African American odyssey. Over the years, several attempts have been made to beautify the cemetery. Westley W. Law spent some five decades trying to preserve Laurel Grove Cemetery South. A plaque records the efforts of the NAACP to preserve the dignity of the cemetery. In the 1960s, Interstate 16 cut the cemetery into two parts. The cemetery was listed on the National Register of Historic Places in 1978, and twenty-two years later, the Georgia Historical Society placed an eight-foot-tall marker at the entrance of Laurel Grove South.

Martin L. King Jr., Boulevard, formerly West Broad Street, was the first paved street in Savannah. As the reign of King Cotton began, Central of Georgia Railroad on West Broad Street became the link between the interior of the state and foreign ports. William Hardee, and the Confederate army crossed the Savannah River on pontoons from West Broad Street to the other side of the River in December of 1864 to escape Sherman's onslaught. In 1892, A. M. Harris, operated a restaurant at Forty-Third and West Broad Streets. The *Savannah Tribune* described the business as "one of the best in the city, furnished neatly and the tables are supplied with the best articles the market affords … Private dining rooms are attached." Harris also ran a hotel at 30 New Street.

Walter S. Scott and six other men, organized the Guaranty Life Insurance Company in Savannah on December 19, 1904. Later, the Scott brothers opened a dry goods store at 462 West Broad Street. By 1954, when Guaranty celebrated its golden anniversary, it had assets of over a million dollars. The company carried the ordinary types of life insurance and hospitalization. A *Savannah Tribune* editorial opined that the success was due to the "patience and business foresight of its organizers and a justification of the confidence its members and friends have imposed in it over the years. It is prophetic of a splendid future."

Mrs. Aurelia E. Allen operated a Colored Millinery Store at 464 West Broad Street. The *Savannah Tribune* claimed that the store was "one of the most completely stocked and highest-class millinery stores operated by Negroes in any city of the Country." It was said to enjoy a "very liberal patronage from all classes of our people." The business also included a "first class dress making department."

Black West Broad Street and the fortunes of black life in general, cannot be understood without reference to segregation. It was segregation, completely rigid by 1920, which created and sustained it. White supremacy was at every turn unsympathetic to the plight of African Americans.

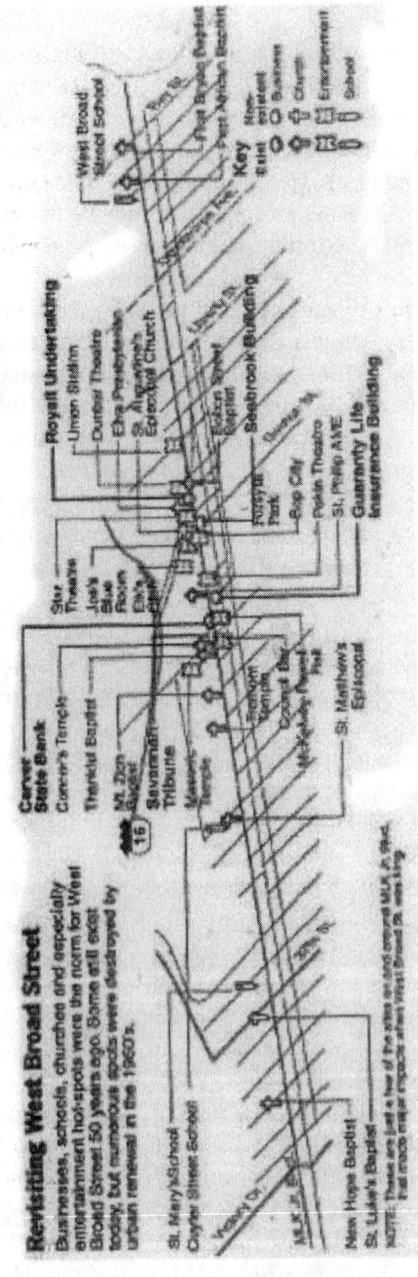

(Courtesy *The Savannah Morning News*)

Sol Johnson, in an editorial in the *Savannah Tribune*, left us his analysis of the "black condition" in 1912:

> Situated as we are, with prejudice, race discrimination and curtailment on every side, our people are now living in the most crucial period in their history. The lines are tightening on us every day. In politics, in business, in religion and every other avenue of activity we find that we are regarded as a separate and distinct people. We are being told in unmistakable terms and most frequently too, that we are not wanted here nor there. The door is closed to us in many places. The so-called square deal has become a shadow in some instances, a memory in others.

Segregation also had the perhaps unintended result of bonding the black community closer together. It was at Union Station that a black man, known simply as Paterson, called out the upcoming stations, in his own unique drawl. West Broad Street had two rail stations and two bus stations. The *Savannah Tribune* regarded the Street as "the second principal retail street in the city," and the black entrepreneurial hub. Many blacks and several Jews, Greeks, and Chinese operated small businesses on West Broad Street.

In 1937, Benjamin F. Hubert made a survey of black businesses in Chatham County. His report stated:

> There are in Chatham County, fifteen barber shops, ten beauty parlors, fourteen cafes and restaurants, nine coal and wood yards, seventy-three confectionaries; five fish and poultry markets, sixteen groceries, six companies doing insurance work—sick, accident and general—one of which has its home office in Savannah; six night clubs; three printing establishments, including two weekly newspapers; six service stations and garages; eighteen shoe repair shops, six funeral homes and undertaking establishments; blacksmith shops; one candy manufacturing concern; three drugstores, one electrical supply shop, one furniture store, two glaziers, one mattress factory, one smoke shop, two real estate dealers and one tailor shop.

The following year Attorney J. G. Lemon reported that black Savannah had one high school, Beach, with 430 students and twelve teachers, and the two junior high schools with 921 students and twenty-one teachers. He found the Negro barbershops still "a thriving small business in all quarters." They were under state regulation and located on the principal streets. There was "little or no competition from white people in this field." Simmons Mattress Company was doing well, supplying blacks and whites with its products. The company made mattresses, pillows and employed a dozen people and operated two trucks. A candy maker sold his goods to retailers. The cleaning, dying and clothing repair shops were doing "a large volume of business," and catered to both races. The two colored weekly newspapers were "well-edited" and were "a credit to the owners and publishers and to the colored people, in that both maintain a high moral and editorial tone and are free of mudslinging practices." Corner musicians and preachers practiced their craft and jazz funerals, in the style of New Orleans, had their day. The *Savannah Tribune* railed against this practice but with little positive effect.

In the trades, blacks had lost ground in carpentry, brick-masonry and painting, due to the rise of white unions. As Lemon reported, "white men are replacing Negro mechanics in much of this work over which colored artisans once had a monopoly." The two black building contractors; however, were holding their own. The two city-qualified master-plumbers and the two certified electrical contractors worked for both races. A large number of men worked as porters and elevator operators in the larger stores and office buildings. Many black women worked in the laundries and the men drove the delivery trucks. The railroads employed "hundreds of colored men as porters, shop helpers, hostlers, switchmen, firemen and track workers." Hundreds more worked in the factories along the Savannah River front, as stevedores and dockhands. In the 1950s, the Street witnessed throngs of people shopping, catching trains at the passenger depots, or seeking entertainment.

Some writers locate the black business section from Oglethorpe Avenue to Gwinnett Street. Clifford Hardwick placed the southern boundary at Anderson Street. According to the *Pettus Savannah Directory* there were 444 black businesses in 1928, 342 in 1930 and 411 in 1940. There were shoe repair shops, photography studios, service stations, cleaners or pressing clubs as they were called, insurance companies, banks, beauty salons, cafés, fruit stands, and pool rooms in the immediate area. Eleven bars and clubs did business between Gwinnett and the present I-16 viaduct. The Masonic Temple was located near Connor's Temple Church. The Afro-American Life Insurance Company, Tom's Grill, the North Carolina Insurance Company, and McKelvey-Powell dance hall were located in the McKelvey building. During the Second World War, the African American USO functioned in the building.

The Bronze Mayor of Savannah. In 1940, the Laymen's League of St. Augustine's Episcopal Church sponsored the contest for the bronze Mayor of West Broad Street. The winner, and his supporting board of aldermen, was expected to "control" the activities "of Savannah's leading Negro thoroughfare." Victory was determined "on the basis of the largest number of votes sold, each five cents reported representing five votes." The Progressives sponsored John (Grapy) Wiley while the Independents supported the popular Carl H. Pugh. Lucius Bryan, Sr., and Arthur Grant were running for City Attorney. Sam Hardy and Tom Washington were competing for City Marshall. Henry Singleton Jr., and Herman Hall were running for Health Officer, Joseph Humes and St. Louis Ponder were contesting for the position of Clerk of Council. The election culminated with a grand ball at the Hollywood Casino. The winner was announced at two o'clock in the morning. John (Grapy) Wiley won the position by over 5,000 votes.

The Wage Earners Loan and Investment Company at West Broad and Alice Streets started in 1900, with total assets of $102. A mass meeting was held at the Ford Opera House on Monday July 8, 1901, at which time the black elite advised the audience on the benefits of supporting a black bank by buying shares. The shares were offered at twelve dollars each. The bank's first offices were located at 22 State Street. Albert Jackson was the first president, but he died only a few months after taking office, and Lucius Williams, the vice-president, became the second President. The bank was chartered by the state in 1913.

As business increased, the decision was made to relocate to 460 West Broad Street. Black

Atlanta builder, Robert E. Pharrow, constructed the $40,000 bank. Pharrow also built St. Philip's A.M.E on West Broad Street. In 1914, the *Savannah Tribune* described the newly built bank as "the most beautiful Negro bank in the Country." That same year George H. Bowen organized the Union Development Corporation to build a structure adjoining the Wage Earners bank.

In 1920, the bank was the first black bank in the country to exceed one million dollars in assets. The *Savannah Morning News* regarded the bank as "the pride of all the people in this community." By 1926, the Wage Earners bank had over 30,000 depositors locally, in other states and overseas. The bank closed in 1928. Sol Johnson, of the *Savannah Tribune,* editorialized, "No greater blow has ever struck our people in this city or state, affecting ones in every walk of life."

The Ralph Mark Gilbert Civil Rights Museum at 406 Martin L. King Jr., Boulevard was opened in 1996 and named for the Rev. Ralph Mark Gilbert, the father of Savannah's modern civil rights struggle. The Museum, rated "Georgia's best" by the *Georgia Journal,* is located in the former Wage Earners Savings and Loan Bank and documents the relentless struggle blacks were subjected to in pursuit of their civil rights.

In 1993, the Beach Institute, the old West Broad Street YMCA on Martin L. King Jr., Boulevard and the former Wage Earners Savings and Loan Bank at 460 Martin L. King Jr. Boulevard competed for the honor of being the location of Savannah's first civil rights museum. The Chatham County's special-option sales tax contributed one million dollars to the project. The Association for the study of African-American Life and History favored locating the museum on Martin L. King Jr., Boulevard.

The Savannah Savings and Real Estate Corporation began operation in October 1915, at a time when there were five black banks in Savannah. Walter Scott, former secretary/treasurer of the Wage Earners Bank, was president of the organization, Paul E. Perry vice-president, and Robert Scott, secretary/treasurer. Towards the end of 1920 the bank began the construction of a new building at 468 West Broad Street. William McKelvey was the builder. After the fall of the Wage Earners Bank in 1928, the Interdenominational Ministers' Union and the Negro Business League held a mass meeting at First African Baptist Church with some 700 persons present, in an attempt to sustain the Savannah Savings Bank, but the bank eventually folded.

The Laborers Investment Corporation, organized in 1917, was located at 515 West Broad Street. The Fidelity Savings located at 626 West Broad Street was organized in 1919. The Mechanics Bank, founded in 1906, had its offices at 20 State Street, then moved to 139 Barnard Street, and finally, to 709 West Broad Street at Maple Street. In 1920, the Mechanics bank had assets of $121,500 and depositors were paid eight percent dividends. Paul Edward Perry was president and S. A. Grant was secretary/treasurer.

Carver State Bank. Louis B. Toomer founded the Georgia Savings and Realty Corporation on February 23, 1927, as a real estate investment and management company in his business place at 505 West Broad Street. He bought out the Howard Stiles Real Estate Company. The combined business was operated at 714 West Broad Street. In 1940, the bank's annual report showed a "big increase" having acquired "about 1,000 in new depositors." The charter was amended and in April 1947, the name was changed to the Carver Savings Bank. In February 1961, the bank moved from 810 Montgomery Street to 918 Montgomery Street.

Toomer was also president of the Commonwealth Investment and the Georgia Savings Investment Company. In 1975, Carver State Bank moved to 701 West Broad Street. Toomer lived at

2711 West Broad Street and owned a successful insurance company and a real estate company. President Eisenhower appointed Toomer Registrar of the U.S Treasury in 1953. Toomer died in 1961, a bronze sundial in Chatham Square at Taylor and Barnard Streets honors him.

John W. McGlockton, of Cuthbert, Georgia, started his grocery in 1936, at the southwest corner of West Broad and Bolton Streets and five years later was regarded as "one of the leading Negro business enterprises of Savannah." Prior to opening his grocery he was in charge of the advertising department of the *Savannah Tribune* for a number of years. He graduated from the Georgia State College and owned his place of business. James Simms had his fish market at West Broad and Walburg Streets, across from Mount Zion Baptist Church. Thomas J. Hopkins had his electrical contracting business at West Broad Street and Walburg Lane. S. L. Mitchell, Hattie Mitchell and Annie Gary owned the Imperial Laundry on West Broad Street between Anderson and Thirty-First Streets. The business, located in a brick building, employed four men and eleven women. It was the largest black owned and operated laundry in the city. One of the owners had worked in the laundry at Savannah State College. Imperial laundered clothes for both blacks and whites but over fifty percent of the jobs came from white people. William C. Sanders conducted a shoe repair business for about nineteen years at 530 West Broad Street.

The Savannah Pharmacy, currently the second oldest black business in Savannah after Bynes Royall Funeral Home, was located at West Broad and Maple Lane. Drs. Earl Fonvielle and Walter Moody began the business in 1914. Ten years later the company had four pharmacies employed five pharmacists, including a female pharmacist, five clerks, two motor delivery men and two porters. The growth of the business was said to be "one of the high spots in local Negro business enterprises." The pharmacy later began the manufacture of ice cream and for a time the drug business was pushed aside. Earl Fonvielle is the third generation Fonvielle still manning the Savannah pharmacy.

Insurance agents leased two stores in the Williams building at 509 West Broad Street and opened the Insurance Agents Department Store in September 1920. The business was capitalized at $100,000 and managed by J. W. McCall. Stocks were ten dollars per share. Thomas McPherson, vice-president of the company was in charge of the grocery department which made deliveries to homes.

The local branch of the National Negro Business League engaged two special pullman cars to take the fifty businessmen to Philadelphia for the 1920 annual meeting of the National Negro Business League. Lucius Williams, president of the Wage Earners Bank and vice-president of the national league, led the delegation. Every "line of business" was represented. There were bankers, brokers, blacksmiths, manufacturers, insurance men, plumbers, lawyers, and physicians. The *Savannah Tribune* reported that blacks in Savannah had more than one million dollars on deposit in the black banks, or an average of forty dollars per person. A year earlier blacks in Chatham County returned for taxation some two million dollars in property, with real property valued at over three million dollars. The total of all Negro property was put at ten million dollars. It was also estimated that the average per capita wealth of Savannah Negroes was two hundred dollars, "a showing which is little short of wonderful." On August 14, 1920, the *Savannah Tribune* boasted that Black Savannah included:

> The Savannah Mattress Company, a Negro "going concern" owns its own home on the city's water front, and manufactures mattresses for all the white furniture houses of the city. There are two hospitals, three drug stores, thirty

Royall Funeral Home
(Courtesy Frank Bynes)

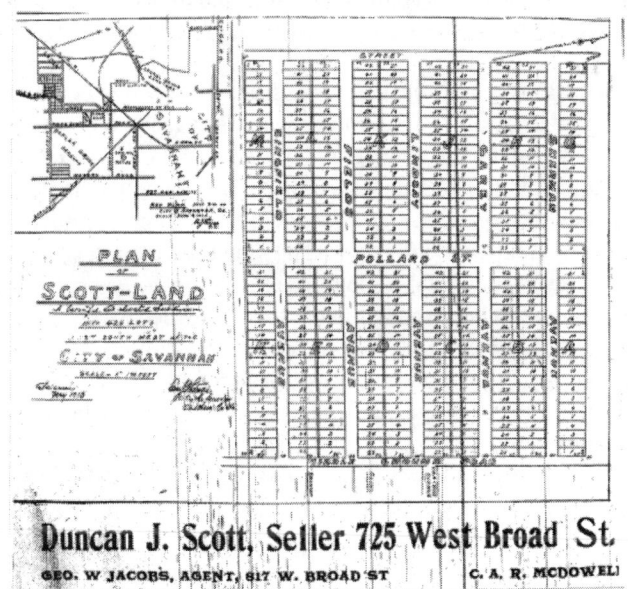

(Courtesy the *Savannah Tribune*)

physicians and dentists, five lawyers, five real estate dealers, four motor-transfer companies, three grain and feed stores and fifteen wood and coal dealers.

There are seventy groceries and butchers, thirty shoe repairing places, ten of which are equipped with modern Goodyear machinery, forty cafés and restaurants, three theaters, two owned by Negroes, twenty-five beauty parlors, two manufacturing their own products and specialties; forty barber shops, two stores which sell gent's furnishings and notions; an automobile accessories supply house carrying a stock of above ten thousand dollars and twenty bicycle and auto repair stations.

There are two weekly news papers, equipped with their own linotypes and power presses. There are eight insurance companies, three of them home companies, with nearly $9,000,000 of insurance in force. There are four principal undertaking companies, with an aggregate of equipment and supplies and stock on hand, all motorized, amounting to seventy-five thousand dollars and doing a total annual business of nearly one hundred fifty thousand dollars.

Royall Funeral Home. William Royall, a prominent deacon at First Bryan Baptist Church, started Royall funeral home. He worked with a white firm carting black bodies away during the yellow fever epidemic of 1876. About two years later, with the financial assistance of Albert Jackson, Royall opened his own coffin and Cooling Board Company at 22½ Whitaker Street. In that day, a three hundred-pound block of ice was placed in a tin container and the body was placed on a board over the ice. Hence the cryptic prayer of our elders: "Thank God when I got up this morning, my bed was not a cooling board."

In 1888, Royall moved his business to 315 South Broad Street, now Oglethorpe Avenue, and added a mutual aid burial society. Seventeen years later the Scott brothers bought the business and later that of Johnson and Fields funeral home. During 1924 Royall Undertaking moved to 501 West Broad Street in the old Globe Theatre building. The building was thoroughly remodeled for about $40,000. The undertaking business was on the ground floor, with a large room for caskets and one room for embalming. The second floor was the living quarters of the "houseman" and his family and the third floor was reserved as a lodge room. The *Savannah Tribune* regarded Royall Undertaking as "one of the most pretentious burial homes in the country owned by a Negro firm." William Pollard was manager and Mrs. Laura Fields was vice-president.

Captain Frank H. Bynes bought the Royall funeral home in 1955. In his youth he had a *Savannah Morning News* route. Some years later he drove a limousine for Sidney Jones Funeral Home and years later he worked for the Royall Funeral Home. At that time Royall also operated an ambulance service. In 1936, Frank Bynes organized a funeral choir and began his apprentice training as an embalmer. The following year he joined the staff of the Coleman mortuary at West Palm Beach, Florida, later becoming the assistant embalmer of the Bethune Funeral Home.

In 1939, Bynes entered the Atlanta Mortuary College, graduating as valedictorian of his class, and passing the Georgia state embalming board with distinction. Frank Bynes joined the U.S. Armed Forces and served in World War II. He later served during the Korean War. Urban renewal forced Bynes to sell the West Broad Street property in 1961 for $26,000. Bynes moved the business to 204 West Hall Street in 1963. In 1989, Wendy's purchased the West Broad Street property for over two million dollars. Presently the Bynes Royall Funeral Home, located at 204 Hall Street, is the oldest black business in Savannah. Frank Bynes informed the author that during the Jim Crow era Royall funeral home was the only local place where blacks could receive practical training in the mortuary business.

Andrew M. Monroe and Company. In 1910, the Monroe funeral home was at West Broad and Charles Streets with its showroom at 605 West Broad Street. It was one of the newer funeral homes and advertised its prices as reasonable "as can be found in the city and a great deal of consideration is always shown to the poor and needy." Toland J. and Essie Monroe Edwards took over the operation of Monroe Funeral Directors. The Monroe block, West Broad Street between Charles and Huntingdon Streets, was destroyed by fire. The undertaking part of the business was rebuilt slightly bigger than the previous entity.

Toland Edwards though born in Savannah, was reared in Boston. He built a penthouse on top of Monroe Funeral Home at West Broad and Charles Streets. The establishment was said to have "the most complete and expensive funeral in Savannah." In 1950, the *Savannah Tribune* reported that three generations of the Monroe family had operated the business.

Captain Edward Seabrook was born in Aiken, South Carolina, in 1869, but came to Savannah in his youth. He became a licensed river pilot, and later opened a new red-pressed brick funeral home at 512-514 West Broad Street, at the corner of West Broad and Minis Streets, which he built for $10,000. The funeral home was on the first floor with a front display room and office, a trimming room, an embalming room and a one hundred seat chapel. In the rear of the building Seabrook built a stable to accommodate his fifteen horses.

Seabrook lived in a penthouse of seven elegantly furnished rooms and a large carriage room in the rear. An elevator for carriage use extended from the first to the second floor. The third floor was divided into two beautiful lodge rooms, "well lighted and well ventilated." The *Savannah Tribune* regarded the building as "the best in the city owned by Negroes." Seabrook later added a "for hire" ambulance service, and owned the first motor powered funeral car owned by a Negro undertaking establishment in Georgia.

Steele Funeral Home. Paul J. Steele received his embalming license January 9, 1909, and went to work for Seabrook Undertaking Company. During World War II, he enlisted in the army and served in France with the Twenty-Fourth Infantry. On his return from the army, he again worked for Seabrook. Steele was the founding commander of Allison Post No. 2933, organized in January 1934. In 1922, he opened his own funeral business at 809 West Broad Street. Later he moved the business to a larger building at 1018 West Broad Street.

In 1926, Steele formed a partnership with Sidney Jones of Sandersville. They conducted business at 511 West Waldburg Street. This partnership was dissolved in 1928. That same year Steele moved his business to the Masonic Temple on West Gwinnett Street. In 1940, Paul Steele moved his funeral home to the Powell building at 714 West Broad Street. The area was described as "the heart of the Negro district."

In 1930, the Peoples' Health and Life Insurance Company merged with the Guaranty Life Insurance Company. The *Savannah Tribune* claimed that the company was one of the state's "largest

Entertainment locations

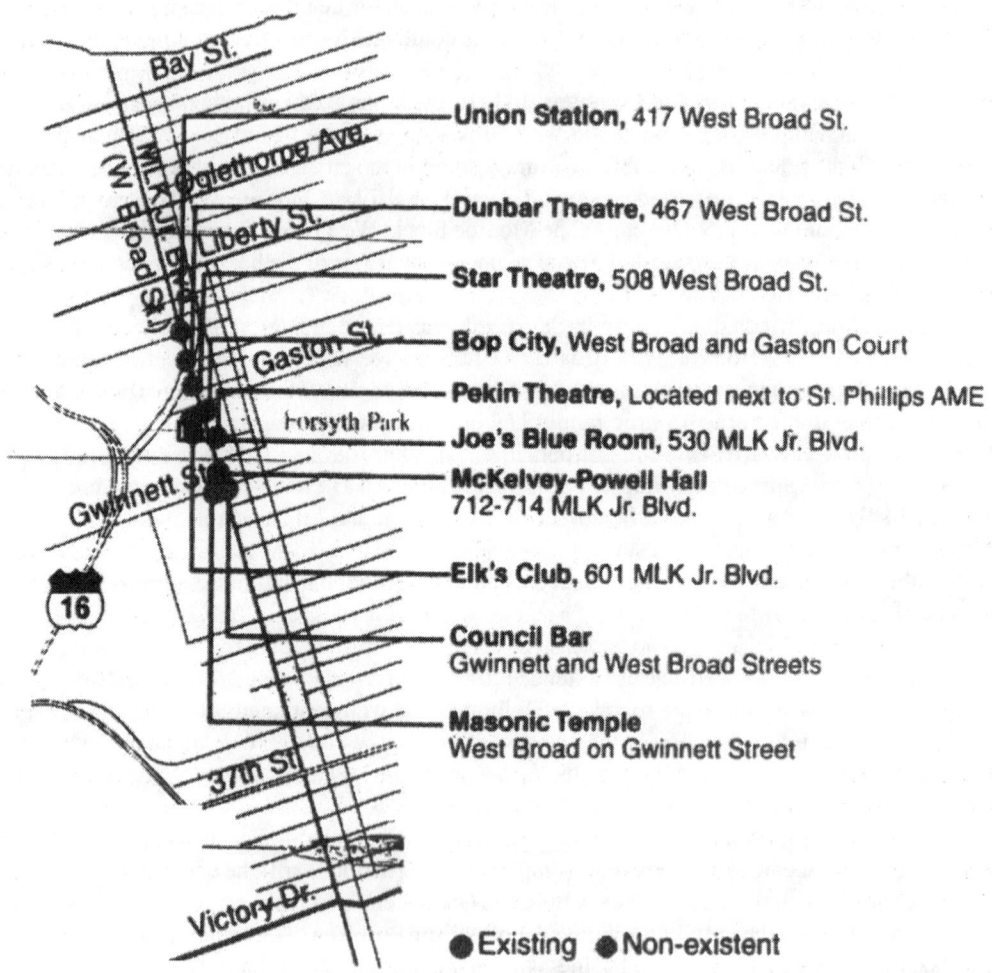

(Courtesy the *Savannah Morning News*)

Negro companies" employing 175 agents, with twenty-five branch offices with assets of $187,232. Guaranty was later sold to Atlanta Life for about $800,000.

Entertainment. Frank Dilworth booked many bands for "gigs" at various clubs. Black musicians could play in white clubs, but black patrons were not allowed to enter white clubs. Al Cutter and Raymond Snype of the Snappy Six performed at all white clubs at Tybrisa, and the USO Club in the McKelvey Powell Building. A housing project now stands where former clubs were located. The Neptune Café opened in 1930 at 811 West Broad Street and soon became "one of the most popular eating places in the colored section." Orich LaMoneda, the proprietor, claimed that the restaurant served "only the best of foods, strictly home cooked." The Café was opened for twenty four hours a day. It was said that many people "made the Neptune Café their regular eating place, and patronage is growing steadily."

Jazz on West Broad Street peaked in the late 1940s and early 1950s. Newer clubs sprang up and pulled the patrons away from the area. Local jazz great, Teddy Adams, thought that the famous West Broad Street "died mainly as a result of integration." In the early 1960s blacks frequented formerly all white clubs and the old black hang-outs petered out. The Hollywood Casino and the Manhattan Club were near Bay Street and Augusta Road. The Coconut Grove Club was on Ogeechee Road where Sam's Club is now located.

Lucius Bryant, Jr., served in the navy in the late 1940s and attended the Boston Conservatory of Music. He later returned to Savannah and opened Lucius Bryant School of Modern Drumming on West Broad Street in a studio above Bop City Night Club at West Broad and Gaston Court. Bryant died in 1963. Joe's Blue Room and Fruit Stand, and the Marine Club were located in the area. Dave's Soda Shop was at 470 West Broad, and Council Bar was at Gwinnett and West Broad Streets. Skipper's Sunset Tavern at 457 West Broad specialized in "beverages, sandwiches and lunches," and was renowned for the "high class food served."

Connie Wimberly and his wife came to Savannah on March 18, 1913, from Birmingham, Alabama, and opened a grocery store in Yamacraw. After seventeen years as a self-employed man, he worked as a Pullman porter. Pop Wimbley's Parlor was on West Broad and Huntington Streets. In 1938, he entered the recreation field with Wimberley's Billiard Parlor at 520 West Broad Street. He was a businessman for more than thirty years. In 1950, Wimberly celebrated thirty-seven years in business. He was then on the board of directors of the Frank Callen Boys Club and vice-president of the local branch of the NAACP. Louise Coffee Shop was next to Wimbley's, and Tom's Grill, Skipper's Sunset Tavern, Curtis Lunchroom, and Alston's Restaurant were all on the street.

Gus Hayes came to Savannah around 1913 from Brooklet, Georgia. In 1936, he operated a small confectionary in West Savannah. Then he opened Gus' Tavern in the 500 block of West Broad Street. Hayes also operated Down Beat and Bop City night clubs at various times. His famous Bop City at West Broad and Gaston Court, offered adult entertainment, and the Flamingo on Gwinnett Street all catered to an almost endless clientele. Hayes closed out his interest in the West Broad Street businesses when he bought the Lincoln Inn at Augusta Road and Bay Street extension. He renovated that building and made it into "one of the most attractive and most successful night clubs in Georgia."

The Dunbar Theater built in 1921 at 467 West Broad Street, was located at the southwest corner of West Broad and Gaston Streets. The building's upstairs hotel, was the only black-owned hotel in Savannah in its day. It was an elegant and popular entertainment center with an orchestra pit, and had live performances by local and national bands. Sam Williams Vanity Shop was housed in the building. In 1928, new equipment was installed "for the showing of pictures with sound and will be the first Negro theatre in Georgia to be so equipped." It featured movies and live "midnight ramblers." Dr. A. P. Williams, Dr. Bryant and Dr. J. W. Jamerson, and the Guaranty Insurance Company occupied the third floor.

The Star Theater on West Broad Street near Gaston Street opened in 1913. The *Savannah Tribune* described the building as "one of the finest in the Country for Negroes." It seated 1200 patrons and was built for about $40,000. A large five-point star with hundreds of colored globes adorned the outside. The ceiling was composed of highly ornamented metal. On the main floor, opera chairs seated 700 and 500 similar chairs were located in the balcony, and standing room for 200 additional people. It was once regarded as the "hottest spot in the city for vaudeville acts and movies." In 1940, B & B Theaters Corporation bought out the business and W. C. Daye became the new manager. Later the theater was damaged by fire and it was torn down in the 1970s. The Scott brothers owned the Star Theater, the Globe Theater, the Scott Brothers Dry Goods, and a real estate firm.

Josephine Stiles Jennings was once described as "Savannah's most active Negro business woman." She started her business career in the late 1890s by opening a meat market and grocery in Yamacraw, then a dance hall at Bay and Fahm Streets. Later she opened Savannah's first Negro Vaudeville hall at West Broad Street, south of Bay Street, then moved back to Yamacraw and opened a saloon with a cabaret upstairs.

She built the Pekin Theater in 1909, at West Broad and Oak Streets. The building originally measured twenty-seven by fifty-two and seated about 300 persons. Two years later a gallery, seating about one hundred persons, was added, and a new front with beautiful electric lights was installed. This structure was demolished and replaced by a new one in 1913, which the *Savannah Tribune* regarded as "one of the most beautiful playhouses owned by Negroes." A modern steam heating plant was installed. The Pekin had its own company to produce Vaudeville one-act comedies, such as "Wash Day in Yamacraw." The theater was in its heyday in the early 1900s.

A fire in 1916 seriously damaged the building but it was immediately rebuilt. Josephine Stiles married Joseph Jennings of Palm Beach, Florida, and returned to the meat and grocery business at Fahm Street, south of Bay Street. Jennings also operated small amusement houses in Jacksonville, Aiken, Brunswick, and Albany. The Pekin closed after the stock market crashed; the building was eventually demolished. Stiles Jennings also owned and operated the Air Dome Theater.

Solomon Charles Johnson, or Sol C. Johnson as he was called, was born in Laurel Hill, South Carolina, in 1866 and came to Savannah as a child. He attended West Broad Street School under Principal James H. C. Butler. After graduating in 1883, Johnson worked in the ruling department of the largest print shop in Savannah and then went to work for John Deveaux's *Savannah Tribune*. When Deveaux was appointed head of customs for the port of Brunswick in 1889, he left the paper in the hands of twenty-three year old Sol Johnson. Johnson bought the business in 1910 at Deveaux's death and remained editor until his death in 1954. In 1908, the *Savannah Tribune* moved to 462 West Broad Street.

Johnson was grand secretary of the Masons, grand patron of the Order of Eastern Star, Adjutant of the First Georgia Volunteers Colored and past officer of Odd Fellows and the Knights of Pythias. He was also the founder and first president of the local Urban League. Johnson was an incredible drum major for his people and an assiduous recorder of the black experience. An editorial in the *Savannah Tribune* on his passing in 1954 stated: "No civic movement within the last fifty years has been projected that did not have his encouragement and moral and financial support."

The *Savannah Journal* was located at 509½ West Broad Street. The publication began in 1918 when Winifred Sherman became editor. He was considered "one of the most finished platform orators in the state and was equally well known for his trenchant pen." Mrs. Rebecca Stiles Taylor edited the paper in 1928, and Melvin Thomas was editor in 1940. John Floyd was publisher and N. G. Morrison was circulation manager. For a short time Prof. Asa H. Gordon also served as editor. The paper's motto was "A paper of the people, by the people, for the people."

Hair styling had always been important to blacks. The *Savannah Republican* of June 6, 1849, regarded the black custom of "dressing up" and the concern about hair styles as almost a "disease." In 1928, Sol Johnson, in a *Savannah Tribune* editorial, recalled the efforts of Charley Bolden, "one of the best known and most popular barbers in the city," to support the state licensing of barbers. Johnson stated that "in past years, nearly ninety-nine percent of the barbers in the city were Negroes who owned most of the larger shops." Ponder's Barber Shop, located at 504 West Broad Street, was regarded as "one of the leading tonsorial establishments among the colored people of the city." Work was done by experts in the barbering trade, and "hot and cold baths" were available in the facility. Barber shops such as Jefferson's Quality Barber Shop, and Lampkin's Deluxe Barber were well patronized.

Then there was Charlie Johnson's Tonsorial Parlor, which served the black community for more than fifty years. Johnson was born in Beaufort, South Carolina, and came to Savannah at age sixteen to attend what is now Savannah State University. He got a job as a porter at Paul Perry's barber shop and stayed in the tonsorial field. Over the years the shop has had several locations. At one time the shop was located at West Broad and Maple Streets. In 1938, Johnson and a former member of the state board of barber and beautician examiners opened a parlor at 705 West Broad Street. The barber shop was also located in the Wage Earners Bank and in the Collier building. Herbert Stevens and Comer Sanders worked with Johnson for more than thirty years each. These were the "in places" for men to have their hair "done."

In 1938, Edward Dye bought the Star Barber Shop on West Broad Street at Duffy Lane from Charlie Warner. The shop was regarded as "one of the most popular tonsorial parlors on the Westside." Dye had engaged in the trade for some fifteen years and was regarded as "one of the best known barbers in the city."

Madam Birdie Freeman, born in Hampton, South Carolina, was "the pioneer among the female hairdressers in Savannah." She came to Savannah in 1903, and in 1914 opened her beauty shop. Her parlor was at 456½ Montgomery Street, and she specialized in the Poro system popularized by Madam C. J. Walker of Indiana, and the Apex College system. In 1939, the Freeman's School of Beauty Culture and Beauty Parlor had Mrs. Catherine Spencer, Mrs. Tena Smith, Mrs. Laura Day, Mrs. Naomi Wilson, Mrs. Lillie Rowe, and Mrs. Marie Holly as Master Beauticians. The facility was enlarged and part of it was used for classes in theory. The *Savannah Tribune* claimed that Madam Freeman held "front rank among the beauticians of this section of the state."

Madam Carrie Cargo, another pioneer in the beauty business, was born in Augusta and graduated from Paine College and studied for one year at Howard University. She came to Savannah and in 1916 opened the Cargo Beauty Salon. Twelve years later she opened the Cargo School of Beauty Culture. Madam Cargo became one of the leaders "in beauty culture in Savannah." She too was a graduate of the Poro system and followed it for some time. Her beauty parlor and school was located at 1219 West Broad Street, at the Northwest corner of West Broad and Henry Streets. It was reported to be "ornate and comfortable." In 1930, Madam Cargo specialized in the "up-sweep" wave. She "completely remodeled and renovated" the building in 1938.

The Cargo School of Beauty Culture employed one instructor and two assistants, while the parlor employed seven graduates. All personnel had to conform to the state regulation governing beauty parlors. These beauty culturists also did nails. A facial massage was done for ten dollars and a manicure for five dollars, while hair weaving went for ten dollars or the total package for twenty-five dollars. A *Savannah Tribune* gossip columnist in the "Lights and Shadows" section in 1936 gave Madam Cargo a compliment by stating "we trust that you will soon eliminate the entire pepper head family so that men will no longer have to go to New York, Chicago, and other places to find a variety of feminine beauty." Another article in the *Savannah Tribune* titled "Look Pretty Please" claimed that the school offered hot oil and scalp treatment for men and women.

Madam Ruth Williams operated her Beauty Salon and College at 815 West Broad Street. She employed ten permanent beauticians and it was said that once a client had her hair done in her studio "you hardly know them when they leave." Her shop specialized in "scalp treatment, skin and facial improvement." Many graduates either established their own shops or worked as operators in other beauty shops around town. In the 1930s, Madam Ruth Williams renovated her facility to accommodate fifty students. The full course cost fifty dollars payable in installments of two dollars down at enrollment and one dollar and fifty cents each week until paid.

Dr. Henry Morgan Collier, Sr., was born in Augusta, June 12, 1889, and came to Savannah in his youth. He did his normal course at Georgia State College and then went to Shaw University in North Carolina. Collier later went to Meharry Medical College and graduated with his M.D. degree in 1913. He practiced medicine for forty-seven years and had his office at 707 West Broad Street.

Dr. Henry M. Collier, Jr., was born in Savannah and graduated from what is now Savannah State University. He later graduated from Meharry Medical College in 1942 and returned to Savannah and practiced medicine for more than forty years. In 1942, he joined his father's practice at 705 West Broad Street. His brother, Dr. Charles Collier, a dentist, graduated from Meharry College School of Dentistry and returned to Savannah where he practiced for forty years. Another brother, Dr. Harold R. Collier, graduated from Meharry Medical College and practiced for eleven years.

Dr. Nathaniel H. Collier, the brother of Dr. Henry M. Collier Sr., graduated from Meharry Medical College Dental School and practiced in Savannah for thirty-two years. The Collier family gave well over 160 years to the medical and dental care of blacks in Savannah.

Dr. J. W. Jamerson, Sr., a graduate of Walden University, now known as Meharry Medical College Dental School, was born in Virginia in 1874. Both his parents died while he was in his youth and he lived with a white family for eleven years. He entered a Presbyterian elementary school and since he had no formal education was placed in the first grade though he was eighteen years of age. Undaunted, Jamerson completed both high school and college and then went to dental school. Dr. Jamerson arrived in Savannah in 1905 and began a practice that was to last for fifty-eight years. His son Dr. J. W. Jamerson Jr., also graduated from Meharry Medical College Dental School, returned to Savannah and joined his father's practice in the Wage Earners Bank at West Broad and Alice Streets. He practiced dentistry for forty-five years.

The present Dr. J. W. Jamerson III, graduated from Howard University Dental School, returned to Savannah and joined his father's practice. He has practiced dentistry for more than twenty years. This family gave well over a century to black dental care and for the past ninety-seven years there has always been a Dr. J. W. Jamerson in Savannah.

Dr. Stephen M. McDew, Sr., was born in Jeff Davis County, Georgia. He later studied at Atlanta University, Walden College and Meharry Medical College where he obtain his M. D. and began the practice of medicine in Ocilla in 1910. In 1923, the family moved to Savannah and Dr. McDew "built up a very lucrative practice." He practiced medicine for forty-five years.

Dr. Stephen M. McDew, Jr., was born in Ocilla, Georgia, and came to Savannah with his family. He was educated at what is now Savannah State University and then went on to study at Meharry Medical College. After graduation in 1939, he completed a two year internship at Hubb Hospital and returned to Savannah and opened an office adjoining that of his father. Both father and son had their offices in the Savannah Pharmacy building at 719½ West Broad Street and worked in the free school clinic of the Federation of Colored Women's Clubs.

Dr. Clarence B. Tyson was born in Monticello, Florida, in 1872. He studied at Talladega College and later at Meharry College in Nashville, Tennessee, where he obtained his M.D., in 1897. He worked for a few years in Waycross then came to Savannah where he established a "large general practice."

His son Dr. William G. Tyson was born in Savannah and graduated from Cuyler Junior High. In 1926, he graduated from Meharry Medical College and returned to Savannah and joined his father's practice in the Wage Earners Bank. Both father and son worked in the free Cuyler School clinics organized by local Federation of Colored Women's Clubs.

William McKelvey organized the McKelvey Services Inc., around 1913 with offices at West Broad and Hall Streets. He was known for his "first class workmanship, architectural skill in designing building projects," and had built up "a reputation second to none in this city." McKelvey did general contracting for both races and built a "wide variety of structures." He constructed more than 300 "modern, up-to-date, completely commodious homes" for blacks and some twenty filling stations for white businessmen. The firm also installed heating, electrical and air conditioning equipment. McKelvey employed a large number of "carpenters, thinners, painters, cement workers, brick masons and plumbers." In addition he operated a modern gasoline station on the premises.

The First African Baptist Church at 23 Montgomery Street on Franklin Square cites several dates as the beginning of its congregation. Sometimes the date 1773 is listed; at other times 1777, but according to yet another source, the date 1788 could also be used. During his more than forty years as pastor, the longest in the congregation's history, Father Andrew Marshall baptized about 3,800, buried 2,040, souls and married over 1,000 couples. Marshall went North to raise funds to build a new church, but died in 1856, in Richmond, Virginia, on his way home.

The First African Baptist Church
(Courtesy the Rev. E.K. Love)

In 1859, during the pastorate of the Rev. William Campbell, a slave pastor, the members built the present brick church, the first brick building built and owned by blacks in Georgia. The bricks were manufactured on site and the women carried them in their aprons to the bricklayers. The members worked on the church after completing the daily tasks of their owners. The walls are four bricks deep and the construction took about four years to complete.

The Rev. Emanuel K. Love was installed as pastor October 1, 1885. During his administration the church reached 5,000 members, and a twenty-six foot addition was added to the rear of the church, at a cost of $18,000. In 1885, the memorial, stained-glass windows commemorating the former pastors, a marble tablet honoring Father Andrew Marshall and a pipe organ were installed. In addition, the church was given a thorough "face-lift." A bronze bell in the tower, weighing 1,067pounds was installed in 1888. The *Savannah Morning News* claimed that the church had "the largest seating capacity of any building in the city." The congregation presented Love with a gold-headed cane. In his first ten years as pastor of the church, Love baptized 1,758 persons and received 187 by letters of transfer. In 1893, a hurricane split the steeple of the church, cutting it down to one fifth of its original height. The congregation never rebuilt this steeple.

Deacon Harry B. James, the church's official tour guide for more than twenty years, took delight in explaining the intricate African designs that the slave builders carved on the gallery pews. The original gopher wood pulpit is now on the ground floor of the church where holes in the floor attest to the presence of a four-foot-deep tunnel which led to the Savannah River and was the conduit for runaway slaves seeking a boat to take them to the North. Most of the lighting fixtures in the sanctuary were converted from the original gas to electricity.

In 1888, when black Baptists celebrated their one hundredth anniversary, a furious debate broke out as to which church was older, First African Baptist or First Bryan Baptist Church. The Rev. Emanuel K. Love, pastor of First African Baptist Church, wrote a book ostensibly proving that his church was the older. Not to be outdone, that same year, the Rev. James M. Simms, a member of First Bryan Baptist, also published his book supposedly proving that First Bryan Baptist Church was the older of the two churches. The definitive conclusion remains moot to this day.

The Rev. Ralph Mark Gilbert became pastor of the church in 1939 and brought new life to the congregation. A social activist, he revitalized the moribund NAACP and led the modern civil rights movement in Savannah. He urged the appointment of the first black policemen in the state, facilitated the establishment of Greenbriar children's home, and black Boy Scout troops. A *Savannah Tribune* editorial at his death in 1956, stated: "Our community lost another of its worthwhile citizens and is poorer because of the passing of one who has meant a great deal to Savannah's Negro community. Indeed the whole community sustains a distinct loss."

During the pastorate of the Rev. William F. Stokes the church underwent a thorough "upgrade." The Rev. Lawrence McKinney opened a museum in the basement. A committee headed by Mrs. Nancy Walker obtained funds from the Georgia Commission for the National Bicentennial Celebration, and the American Revolution Bicentennial Administration. The church's museum displays portraits of the seventeen pastors of the church and, among other items, a communion bread tray donated by the women of the church in 1814.

Courtesy of Pastor T.N. Tillman & Congregation

The Savannah River

In 1767, the British authorities bought 104 acres and built a lazaretto, or quarantine station, near the entrance of the Savannah River. All boats with slave cargoes had to stop at the lazaretto and the sick were kept in the hospital while those who had died were buried nearby. All other slaves were "prepared" by oiling them, for example, and sent to Savannah for sale.

Colerain Plantation was located seven miles west of the city. In the early days over 300 slaves made bricks and planted and ginned cotton on the plantation. James Simms and his family were slaves on this plantation. Today it is the home of the Sugar Refinery,

Mulberry Grove Plantation was twelve miles northwest of Savannah. Eli Whitney in 1793 "invented" the cotton gin here. According to Jefferson Hall, Whitney "perfected" a previously invented cotton gin. This invention helped trigger the expansion of slavery, American industrialization and the Civil War. It also devastated the top soil. The Georgia Ports Authority is now on the general location.

Hermitage Plantation three miles east of Savannah was an industrial plantation. By 1820, Henry McAlpin, and his hundreds of slaves, made bricks, and operated the earliest railway in the country to move the bricks to kilns. He manufactured the rails in the iron foundry on the plantation. The slaves made thousands of bricks which now grace many mansions in downtown historic Savannah, the Central of Georgia station, Fort Pulaski, and the embankments in the rear of the station. These bricks also bear silent witness to the black hands that made them. International Paper Company now occupies the general area of this plantation.

Brampton Plantation on the Savannah river near New Yamacraw was the first location of "Old Jerusalem," that inchoate congregation, with which five contemporary African American congregations are connected. The venerable Andrew Bryan and his family were slaves on that plantation.

The Savannah River became the entrance point for the slave sawyers loaned to Oglethorpe by Thomas Broughton, for whom Broughton Street is named, Thomas and Ann Drayton, for whom Drayton Street is named, and Colonel Bull for whom Bull Street is named. These slaves helped the colonists to fell trees and layout the town. Later the river became the commercial hub of King Cotton and canoes or Indian trade boats plied the waterways.

The forty foot high bluff on the river bank had rows of connected buildings housing cotton and later naval stores. The upper level contained the offices of cotton factors, or brokers. Factors' Walk was at the center of this complex. In 1867, black stevedores struck when the city increased the cost of work badges from three to five dollars. The leaders were arrested, fined fifty dollars and jailed.

Hundreds of blacks worked on the river as pilots, stevedores, boat hands or servants. Logs of pine and cypress were floated down river as Savannah became the lumber capital of the Atlantic coast. Free colored seamen plied their trade throughout the Atlantic and Caribbean waters. From 1803 to 1829 about fifteen percent of the seamen in the Savannah port were black. George Baker, alias Father Devine, according to one story, was born on Hutchinson Island and after a few years "went North," where he became a prominent religious functionary during the 1920s and 1930s, and did much to advance the lot of blacks.

German Captain Herman Sengstacke on one of his trips from Bremen, Germany, to Savannah saw Tama, a young female slave, on an auction block in 1847, bought her and subsequently married her. On Tama's death, the Captain sent his two children to be educated by relatives in Germany. In 1869, the son John, returned to Savannah and found a position as a German translator for the *Savannah Morning News*. When the paper discovered that Sengstacke was black he lost his job. Young Sengstacke became a Congregational minister and eventually married Flora Abbott, the mother of Robert Abbott, the founder of the *Chicago Defender*. That paper, the first black daily in the nation, had a tremendous influence on the exodus of blacks from the South to the North.

John H. Deveaux, a colored teenager, and Moses Dallas, a former slave pilot who in 1864 gained his freedom, were involved in the attempt to capture the United States gunboat the Water Witch. Pilot Dallas guided the Confederates "over the treacherous sandbars successfully and came up with the Union vessel at anchor in the Ossabaw Sound." One story has it that Dallas died in the mêlée. Another narrative reports that he escaped and later joined the Union navy. Black seaman McIntosh jumped ship and swam to shore where he was picked up by the Union side.

Anthony Desverney was born in Charleston, South Carolina, in 1831, but lived most of his life in Savannah. In 1877, he was listed as a "colored cotton shipper" with his business at 84 Bay Street. He was reputed to be the "wealthiest Negro in Savannah." Desverney was an Adjutant of the colored troops, and at his death the *Savannah Tribune* reported, "There has not been a death in a long while to have caused so much general sorrow as was the demise of Adjutant Anthony K. Desverney."

Captain John H. Newton was born in Savannah, June 19, 1863. During the First World War he served on the SS City of Memphis. In 1961, Newton, who lived at 511 East Jones Street, celebrated his ninety-eighth birthday. He worked on the river for half a century, and received his certificate from the Coast Guard. He served as a deputy sheriff of Chatham County for more than fifty years and also as a Notary public.

Captain John Starr was born in Bryan County in 1865, but came to Savannah a few years later and entered the revenue cutter service in 1898. He worked on boats for many years and in 1902 he was a licensed pilot of steam vessels for the district of Savannah. Starr piloted the Coast Guard Cutter Yamacraw in her maiden voyage up the Savannah River in June 1909. Starr was a member of the Spanish American War Veterans. He later served as a block warden in the local Civilian Defense unit.

The African American Monument. In 1991, Dr. Abigail Jordan, one time professor at Savannah State University, conceived the idea of erecting a monument on River Street in honor of the life and labor of African Americans in Savannah. Sculptor Dorothy Radford Spradley, a professor at the Savannah College of Art and Design, was chosen for the project and started working on it in 1995. The 703 pound, larger than life, bronze statue, depicts an African American family of four with broken shackles near their feet. The Elberton gray twenty-two thousand pound granite base bears the words of poet Maya Angelou.

On July 27, 2002, after eleven years of much strife and struggle, the monument on Rousakis Plaza behind City Hall, was dedicated in the presence of some three hundred persons. Dr. Jordan pledged one hundred thousand dollors of her own money to finance the project. The city council paid for the site preparation and seating near the monument.

The Trustees Garden was a ten acre experimental agricultural station in early Colonial times. By 1751, only a few trees were left. The Herb House was built around 1858. Quamino Dolly who aided the British owned property on this spot.

Bay Street. The 33rd. U.S. Colored Troops came in along this route with General Sherman's troops and helped occupy the city.

The Vietnam Monument is sculptured in the shape of the country was erected in 1990. The names of the 106 black and white Chatham County personnel lost in battled are inscribed on the slab.

The Cotton Exchange was designed by William Preston in the Romanesque Revival style. It opened in 1887 and closed in 1920. The labor of slaves made this enterprise possible.

The Custom House was designed by John Norris and completed in 1852. It was Savannah's first iron construction and fireproof building. There Savannah born Supreme Court Associate Justice James Moore Wayne presided over the case of Charles Lamar and the ship Wanderer in 1859. President William McKinley appointed John H. Deveaux inspector of customs for the port of Savannah in 1898 and he remained in that position until his death in 1909.

City Hall. Hyman Witcover designed this building which was built in 1905. In 1995, Floyd Adams Jr., became the first African American elected mayor of Savannah.

Downtown Savannah. A decree published in 1790 stipulated that slaves must live with their owners. Some slaves lived on the ground floor, in the lanes behind the owners' houses or over their carriage houses. The present Owens-Thomas carriage house and slave quarters at 124 Abercorn Street, is an example of this dispensation. A slave could receive thirty lashes on the back for not living with his owner. In reality, however, many slaves "lived out," that is, away from their owners' immediate premises. In 1798, about one quarter of the slaves lived on the edges of the town.

By 1848, one fifth of all slaves lived in the Oglethorpe ward and many wards had an equal number of both races. At one time about sixty percent of Savannah's slaves lived away from their owners. Throughout the period about twenty-five percent to fifty percent of each ward was black. Many of Savannah's antebellum mansions are mute witnesses both to the labor of the slaves who helped build them and their labor in the cotton fields which was the foundation of white wealth. In one sense, Georgia's motto, *non sibi sed aliis,* not for us but for others, applied more to the slaves than to their owners.

Some free coloreds built their homes on the eastside of downtown Savannah. In 1810, the Rev. Henry Cunningham, founding pastor of Second African Baptist Church, built his home at 117-119 Houston Street opposite the church. Charlotte and William Hall built their home in 1818 at 519 East President Street. The Savage family built their home in 1852 at 228 West Gaston Street and F. A. Mirault built his home at 508 East Gordon Street. The 500 block of York Street, as well as around Greene Square, contained many homes owned by free coloreds. Simon Mirault built at 21 Houston Street. Anthony K. Desverney built his home at 540-42 East Taylor Street. Mosianna Milledge, Juliette Gordon Low's famous cook, had her home at 513 East Gaston Street. Catherine and Jane

Second African Baptist Church

Interior of Second African Baptist Church
(Courtesy the *Savannah Morning News*)

Deveaux's house was located on St. Julian Street. John Barlow built at 517-519 East President Street. The Sabatie family built at 509 East Charlton Street. In 1860, Savannah had 705 free people of color, the largest number in the state.

According to W. W. Law, in the early 1900s, working class blacks were removed from down town Savannah and the houses they lived in were replaced by gardens. The present "look" of downtown Savannah "misrepresents" the previous black presence in the area.

Second African Baptist Church at 123 Houston Street on Greene Square was founded by the Rev. Henry Cunningham, and a group of mostly free people of color, on December 26, 1802. The original group included John B. Deveaux, the church's first deacon, Thomas Anderson, Scipio Gordon, Richard Houston, Betsey Cunningham, the pastor's wife, Silvia Whitefield, Silvia Monax, Charlotte Walls, Leah Simpson and Susan Jackson. The first church building was "a one-level structure over a shallow basement." Cunningham pastored the church for forty years.

Cunningham was implicated in the 1829 discovery of David Walker's "Appeal to the Colored man ..." Walker, a former North Carolina slave, escaped to the North and wrote his pamphlet encouraging blacks to snatch their freedom from their owners. One story claims that Cunningham received sixty copies of the paper from a seaman on board one of the ships docking on the waterfront and passed on the material to the mayor.

On the evening of February 2, 1865, Major General Rufus Saxon addressed a church meeting of over 1,000 blacks and explained the implications of General Sherman's Special Order #15 granting abandoned Confederate lands from South Carolina to Florida, to the former slaves. This meeting in Savannah gave birth to the famous "forty acres and a mule" story. Each family was promised forty acres and a mule that the Federal forces no longer needed. The Rev. Ulysses Houston, pastor of First Bryan Baptist Church, led 1,000 blacks to Skidaway Island and laid out his settlement.

During the pastorate of West Indian born, the Rev. Alexander Ellis, a remarkable remodeling was done to the church. The one story wooden building constructed in 1802 was raised fourteen feet and placed on a brick basement. The second floor, nineteen feet high, was added together with a balcony and an indoor baptismal pool, the first in a black church in Savannah. As the *Savannah Tribune* stated "the new edifice owes its being to the energy of its pastor Rev. Alexander Ellis, one of the ablest and most eloquent divines in the country."

Stained-glass windows and cushioned pews were added. In 1890, the church petitioned the court to remove the word African from its title. That same year, the Rev. Alexander Ellis split the congregation into two parts giving rise to Beth Eden Baptist Church. Around 1910, the choir loft was moved from the rear balcony to its present position facing the congregation.

The church suffered severe fire damage in February 1925 and the wooden exterior was replaced with red brick veneer and the stained glass windows were also replaced. An air conditioning unit was installed in the 1950s. Members claim that the Rev. Dr. Martin L. King, Jr., gave a portion of his "I Have a Dream" speech in the church during 1963. Some windows were added in 1977 and a museum was planned for the third floor. In the 1980s the charter was renewed and the word African was reinserted into the church's name. In 1999, Deacon Curtis V. Cooper headed a committee which raised funds and upgraded the entire facility added an elevator and a new public address system.

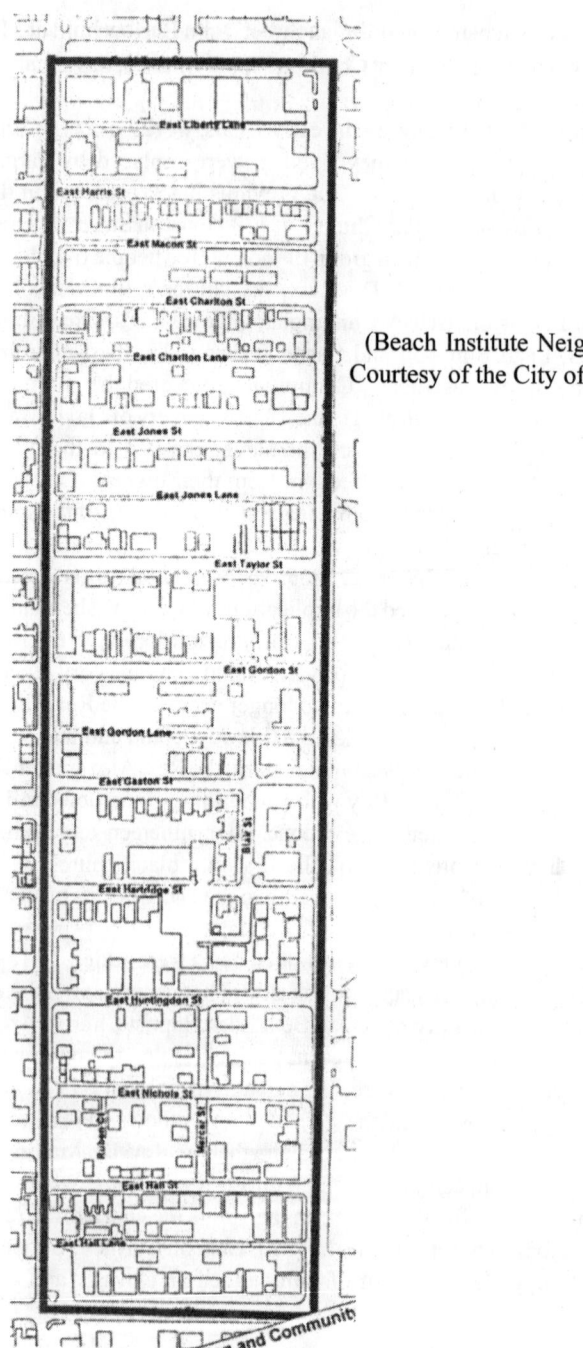

(Beach Institute Neighborhood
Courtesy of the City of Savannah)

The second floor sanctuary was also restored for a total of about $400,000. This congregation celebrates its two hundredth anniversary in December 2002.

Beach Institute Neighborhood in the Southeastern corner of the National Historic Landmark District is comprised of eleven blocks, thirty-three acres bounded by East Liberty, East Broad, East Gwinnett and Price Streets. The area takes its name from the Beach Institute. In Colonial times it was the estate of Sir James Wright, the last British governor of Georgia. In 1782, the area was called Fairlawn. The arrival of the Savannah-Albany railroad complex in the 1850s ushered in new housing for racially-mixed railroad workers. A few blacks owned property in the area before the Civil War.

Several black carpenters such as Robert Low Bullock of 520 East Jones Street, and James R. Middleton at 521 Hartridge Street, lived in the area. The Silas Fulton family built the brick houses at 505-507 and 509-511 East Jones Street. In the 1870s the district gradually changed to an all-black neighborhood. St. Benedict's Church built in the 1870s, St. John's Baptist Church built in 1891, and St. Francis Convent built in 1908, all helped to stabilize the locality. At one time the area was considered a black middle class neighborhood.

Beach Institute at 502 East Harris Street at Price Street was built by the American Missionary Association and the Savannah Educational Association in 1867 for the education of black children. The Institute was named for Alfred E. Beach, editor of the *Scientific Magazine,* who donated funds to purchase the land. Blacks contributed to the building of a teachers' hostel in the rear of the Institute. Beach was a public school from 1874 to 1878 when it was damaged by a mysterious fire. That year, the A.M.A regained control of the school. In 1917, the Savannah Boys Club met in its basement. Two years later, a rumor was afloat that Beach Institute would be closed. The *Savannah Tribune* editor Sol C. Johnson was shocked at the news because:

> Beach has stood like a sturdy oak for half a century to shelter those who sought her ministrations. Like a mighty lighthouse to save and succor those who struggle to find their way like the light house Beach has turned the steps of many a wavering soul into the path of definiteness and certain goal.

Beach Institute finally closed as a school in 1970. Nine years later the Board of Education sold the building to the Savannah College of Art and Design which subsequently donated the building to the King-Tisdell Cottage Foundation. Over 200 of Ulysses Davis' wood carvings are on permanent display in Beach Institute. Davis was born in Fitzgerald, Georgia, but lived in Savannah for more than forty years. A railroad blacksmith and barber, Davis from the age of ten, had a passion for carving wooden images. Dr. Virginia Kiah, a local black artist, "discovered" Davis in 1953. His work toured the country in 1982 and was displayed in the Library of Congress.

St. Stephen's Episcopal (Unitarian Church) congregation was established by William Claghorn and others in the winter of 1855. By 1860, needing a larger facility, the congregation bought the John Norris-designed unused Unitarian church on Oglethorpe Avenue, and moved it on rollers to Troup Square. James Pierpont, brother of the pastor and organist of the church composed the famous "Jingle Bells." According to Eleanor "Nellie" Pollard, the members of St. Stephen's did the work of adapting the building to the requirements of the Episcopal liturgy.

In 1871, the Board of Education took over St. Stephen's Episcopal Church's private school, rented the facility, and opened the first public school for blacks in Savannah in the unused rectory at 313 East Harris Street. Some months later a mysterious fire damaged the building and the school was transferred to the Scarbrough House on West Broad Street. In the 1940s, St. Stephen's congregation sold the building to white Baptists. Forty-nine years later and after a break of 137 years, on Easter Sunday, March 30, 1997, the Unitarian Congregation re-took possession of the church and spent more than two million dollars in renovating the building.

Frank Callen's Boys and Girls Club was organized by Frank Callen, a newly appointed probation officer of the Juvenile court, on October 19, 1917. The club, originally called the Savannah Boys' Club, was located in the basement of Beach Institute, and aimed to provide recreation and vocational guidance to underprivileged boys less than seventeen years old. The club became a charter member of the Boys Clubs of America July 5, 1922. In 1929, the club bought the McDonough estate at Charlton and Price Streets for $11,000. Mrs. Sarah Hodge, the "angel of Savannah," donated liberally to this cause. She had her famous Christmas party for the children each year. Former member Sam Parker, Sr. recalls that as a youngster he presented a handkerchief to Mrs. Mills Hodge as her Christmas present from the boys club.

In 1932, about 723 boys received training in shoemaking, tailoring, carpentry and painting. Five years later, Frank Callen was awarded the bronze bar by the National Boys Club of America for twenty years of "outstanding service." The following year the Boys Club became a charter member of the reorganized Community Chest. In 1939, he took over the operation of the club. Callen died in 1949. The club's name was changed from the Savannah Boys Club to the Frank Callen Boys Club, and his wife Mrs. Irma Callen became director. A retired school teacher, she had held the post of assistant director. The Club at 330 Price Street was demolished and a new $80,000 building was constructed. The Savannah Foundation, Inc., donated liberally to this cause. The club had temporary facilities in the old Bethlehem Center at 436 Price Street.

In 1978, Westley W. Law and others tried to save this black neighborhood. Ten years later the city approved loans to the Beach Neighborhood Association to renovate or remove buildings. Later, over five million dollars were pumped into the area. A recent study of the area found that only eleven percent of the dwellings were owner-occupied.

The King-Tisdell Cottage at 514 East Huntington Street, a small Victorian cottage with intricate gingerbread adornments was built in 1896 for W. W. Aimer. Eugene Dempsey and Sarah King bought the building in 1910. After her husband's death in 1941, Mrs. King married Robert Tisdell. The building was slated for demolition as part of the urban removal project in the Wheaton Street area. Westley W. Law and members of the Savannah-Yamacraw chapter of the Association for the study of Afro-American Life and History began the struggle to save the buiding. The city of Savannah contributed money toward the renovation of the building. The Historic Savannah Foundation bought a lot on Huntingdon Street and donated it to the Beach Institute. The King-Tisdell house was then moved to the Beach Institute neighborhood at 514 Huntingdon Street. In July of 1981, the building was opened as a cultural museum of African American arts and crafts and

St. Stephen's Episcopal Church
(Courtesy St. Matthew's Collection)

Beach Institute

King-Tisdell

(Courtesy Beach Institute)

houses many old documents such as the Emancipation Proclamation and General William Sherman's Field Order #15. The basement contains many household memorabilia that an average black middle-class household would have had between 1874 and 1950.

Old Fort. There is no consensus on the exact boundaries of this section of Savannah. Some authors center it in the former Trustees Garden along the Bluff and east of East Broad Street. Others extend it from the river to Liberty Street and from Randolph to Habersham Streets. One even claims that "Washington square and by the gas works was the real Old Fort." A more recent study declares, that the area is bounded by the Savannah River, the old Coca-Cola plant and Liberty and Price Streets, the northeastern section of Savannah. The name probably came from the eighteenth century Fort Wayne, or an earlier fort, which guarded the harbor from the bluff at Bay and East Broad Streets. Most writers agree however, that the area was a "rough and tumble" section of the city.

In the 1840's the Irish shared this cosmopolitan area with "Blacks, Italians, Germans, and Greeks." The houses were described as unpainted "one-story frame structures." Many black inhabitants were Gullah people from South Carolina who brought their customs with them. Some were experts at basket weaving, woodcarving and above all they had a strong sense of their African heritage. Crawford Square bonfires on New Year's Eve were very popular, as were the games, "Pluffer," "half Rubber" and "Georgia skin." The area peaked as a cohesive and viable black community in the early 1900s. Walter Scott, in a letter to the editor of the *Savannah Morning News* in 1958, stated, "In changing the occupancy of this area (Yamacraw) from Negro to white, the city is following the pattern used in the Old Fort where hundreds of Negro families were removed and replaced by white families."

Urban renewal, or as some called it, black removal, in the late 1940s displaced many residents. The poorest homes were in Tin City behind Jones Old Field which sprouted during the Depression. In 1932, Tin City was described as "a Negro colony of tiny huts constructed of scraps of tin and other material from the dump heap." Some homes were "one room structures with hardly enough head room for a man to stand upright." Each house had its vegetable garden.

The West Broad Street School/Scarbrough House. William Jay designed this house for William Scarbrough and it was built in 1819. Scarbrough owned 100,000 acres and 400 slaves in South Carolina. In 1878, George Wimberly Jones DeRenne donated the building to the Board of Education for the education of black children in gratitude for the work their ancestors contributed to the advancement of Savannah. A codicil in the deed stipulated that whites could be educated in the school if the time ever came that there were no blacks in the city. Principal James H.C. Butler, his wife Mrs. Sarah Flemister Butler, and Miss Alice Miller, their friend from undergraduate days at Atlanta University, all lived in the same house on Henry Street, and taught at West Broad Street School for a total of some 140 years.

Yamacraw on the west side of Martin L. King Jr., Boulevard, south of the Savannah River to the canal and south to Hull Street, is one of the oldest black neighborhoods in the city. The Yamacraw Indians lived on the bluff west of English settlement until 1735 when they moved to Pipemakers Creek. In the mid 1800s German and Polish Jews, Irish and others, joined blacks in the area, perhaps because of its cheap rent, and the Irish and blacks often competed against each other for the same jobs. Many Gullah people settled in the area. During slavery times the area was almost

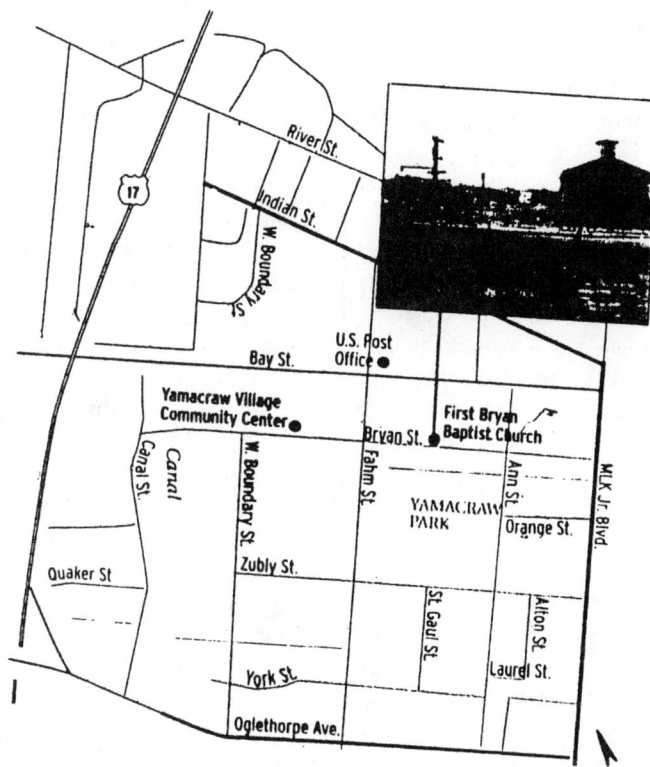

(Courtesy the *Savannah Morning News*)

(Courtesy The Housing Authority of Savannah)

a sanctuary for runaway slaves. James Weldon Johnson in his work "Go down Death" states, "And God said: Go down, Death, go down, down to Yamacraw and find Sister Caroline." At one time the locale was described as, "a swampy area in the Northwest formerly inhabited by free Negroes." Root doctors and "cunjur" experts plied their trade with such remedies as "Mojo Incense" to return lost love.

In 1928, Mrs. Sarah Mills Hodge, a white philanthropist who supported many black endeavors, purchased 610 Bay Street West and converted it into a kindergarten in memory of her husband Henry Hodge. The building was thoroughly renovated and "equipped with every modern convenience." Forty kindergarten children, from three weeks to four years, occupied the ground floor. Mrs. Lucille Baldwin Spencer Johnson was head teacher of the school for thirty-nine years. Johnson studied at Beach Institute and obtained her normal diploma from Atlanta University. She did further study at Columbia University and Cheyney State Teachers College. Mrs. Maria Shefftal Jackson was her assistant. Head nurse Miss Carrie B. Tolbert and Miss Ida Lee, R. N., her assistant, operated an infirmary three blocks from the kindergarten, at 550 Orange Street. Miss Lee graduated from the Georgia Infirmary Training School for Nurses and also did private nursing for many years. She was a graduate of the Poro College of Scalp Treatment and Hair Culture.

In 1937, President Benjamin F. Hubert of the Georgia State College recorded the fact that Mrs. Franklin Roosevelt knew of Yamacraw. The area had sixty blocks of houses, mostly "frame structures in poor repair and in great need of paint." The houses were generally "dilapidated, unpainted and crowded" and the area was once known as the "toughest section" in Savannah. The houses were built close together, on narrow streets. Very few houses had modern conveniences, such as electricity, and running water and the neighborhood was thickly populated. Hubert estimated that ninety-eight percent of the people living there were Negroes, and that a few white people operated most of the stores and markets at the corners of the main streets. The people were "proud of Yamacraw. They are proud of their neighbors."

In the early 1900s Savannah was famous for its gambling houses which attracted many tourists who came more to gamble in the casinos on the outskirts of the city, than to enjoy the sights. Many people, especially blacks, played the numbers games in "policy shops," and organized bolita games. A dime ticket offered a chance to win seven dollars and fifty cents and a dollar ticket in a "10-piece" could win seventy-five dollars. On Saturday nights "Cuba" took over from the bolita since the payoff was higher. It was based on the Cuban lottery. This underground economy also included a fair amount of bootlegging and houses of prostitution. The ones on Indian Street were more famous than those on Montgomery and West Broad Streets.

The dilapidated houses at the city's entrance were deemed an eyesore and by the 1940s urban renewal changed the neighborhood. The slum clearance called for the demolition of 702 houses and the construction of 480 new units. C.W. Angle Inc., of Greensboro, was the contractor. The city's Housing Authority administrative building was modeled after the "big house" at the Hermitage plantation. In 1969, the people of Yamacraw took to the streets to protest the heavy truck traffic which passed through the neighborhood. Mayor Curtis Lewis suggested abandoning the area. Eventually a series of one-way streets was adopted. The area had a "makeover" in the 1990s. The complex was reduced by ninety units and parking lots were added.

St. Philip Monumental A.M.E.
(Courtesy Year Book of Colored Savannah)

Bethlehem Missionary Baptist
(Courtesy Bethlehem Collection)

First Bryan Baptist
(Courtesy the *Savannah Morning News*)

The First Bryan Baptist Church at 575 West Bryan Street in Yamacraw claims 1788 as its beginning. Father Andrew Bryan and his followers were whipped by their fellow Christians and suffered much persecution in their quest for religious freedom. In 1789, Bryan bought his freedom and later that of his wife and daughter and in 1793, the lot on which the church is now located. By 1800, the congregation reached 800 souls and was accepted as a respectable part of Savannah's religious milieu. Bryan was "loved and honored by white and black." He was the last of the original fathers to come from the banks of the Savannah River. When he died in 1812, over 5,000 persons attended his funeral. The Rev. Andrew Marshall succeeded his uncle as pastor of the church. The congregation became known as the First Colored Church and in 1822 changed the name to First African Baptist Church. In 1826, Lowell Mason of the Independent Presbyterian Church started a Sunday school at First Bryan Church. After some years Bryan's members took over the school.

During the pastorate of Father Andrew Marshall the congregation moved to Franklin Square and a "battle royal" broke out over the "new theology" of human brotherhood, preached by the Rev. Alexander Campbell. A small group (155 persons) led by West Indian born Deacon Adam Arguile Johnson broke away and returned to the original location at 575 West Bryan Street. Father Andrew Marshall headed the larger part of the congregation (2,640 persons) housed in the former white Baptist church on Franklin Square.

A year after the 1832 split, the present Bryan Baptist Church constituted themselves as the Third African Baptist Church. Deacon Johnson died March 19, 1835, having served his church for some forty years. The Rev. Ulysses Houston was installed as pastor in 1861 and remained pastor until he died in 1889, the longest pastorate in the church's history. The church records indicate that the years 1836 to 1916 qualified as, "a period of struggle." The church was charted by the state of Georgia in 1866 and incorporated the following year, taking the name First Bryan Baptist Church in honor of Father Andrew Bryan.

In 1871, there was a second split as the Rev. Alexander Harris and forty-five members separated themselves from the congregation, moving to West Broad Street at Waldburg Street, where they established another First Bryan Baptist Church. The present First Bryan Baptist Church, a limestone stucco and brick, Corinthian-style, two-story church, was designed by John B. Hogg, and built by the members in 1873. The church measured seventy-five feet long and fifty-six feet wide and forty-five feet high and cost $30,000. A pipe organ was bought from the Presbyterian Church for $1,350.

In 1916, the congregation erected a monument in front of the church, in honor of the Rev. George Liele. The spelling on the monument lists his name as George Lisle. Additions to the facility were made in 1945, and in 1956, an educational annex costing $25,000 was added. In 1978, the church received historic landmark status and a historic marker was placed on the premises. Father Andrew Bryan is memorialized by a stained-glass window. Other stained-glass windows were installed in 1987.

In 1988, the church celebrated its bicentennial by opening the cornerstone. The metal box contained more than 400 coins from different countries, some dating from the 1700s; leather bound bible, and jewelry. Some 150 members, and the Rev. Edward Ellis, gathered at Bryan's grave in Laurel Grove Cemetery South to remember their founder. In 1994, a proposal was made to transform Wessels Plaza, opposite First Bryan Baptist Church, into a $300,000 art park commemorating the groups who lived in the area. Jerome Meadows designed the art park.

St. Phillip's Monumental A.M.E., Georgia's oldest African Methodist Episcopal congregation was founded in 1865. In 1820, the white Methodists built a meeting house for their black members, and in 1845 they built Andrew Chapel for the use of blacks. In 1865 the black members of Andrew Chapel egged on by the Rev. Bradwell and the Rev. James Lynch, "made secret arrangements" to take Andrew Chapel into the African Methodist Episcopal denomination as a body. They built a church on Hull Street and took the name St. Phillip's A. M. E. Church. The Rev. Henry M. Turner served as pastor of the church in 1872.

In 1893, a hurricane toppled the steeple but it was rebuilt. Six years later a second hurricane, with a seventy-five mile an hour wind surge lasting fifty minutes, killed sixteen persons, and damaged about 1,000 buildings. The wind knocked down St. Phillip's steeple and it crashed into the body of the church. The 1,400 members split into three parts. One section rebuilt on the same site, another built on West Broad Street in 1914, and a third part joined the Colored Methodist Episcopal denomination

Images of Black Savannah

Planting rice -(Courtesy of Liveoak Public Libraries)

Blacks working on the fortifications of Confederate Savannah
(Couresy of Liveoak Public Libraries)

The Rev. Andrew Cox Marshall
(Courtesy of the Rev. E. K. Love)

The Rev. Alexander Harris
(Courtesy of the *Savannah Tribune*)

The Rev. James Merilus Simms
(Courtesy of the *Savannah Tribune*)

Col. John H. Deveaux
(Courtesy of the *Savannah Tribune*)

Sol C. Johnson, Editor *Savannah Tribune*, 1889-1954.
(Courtesy of the *Savannah Tribune*)

The Staff of the *Savannah Tribune*
(Courtesy of the *Savannah Tribune*)

Col John H. Deveaux

Adjutant Sol C. Johnson

Lieut. Julius Maxwell

Lieut J.C. Williams

Sergt. R. W. Spaulding

(Courtesy of the *Savannah Tribune*)

Lieut. Robert Campbell

(Courtesy of the *Savannah Tribune*)

Paul J. Steele

Corporal James J. Edwards,
awarded the French
Croix de Guerre and Star

Dr. Wilmette & Martha Wilson
(Courtesy of Martha Wilson.)

Josie Mae Smith
(Courtesy of Olivia Swanson)

Lula Brown Johnson
(Courtesy of Dr. Lester Johnson, Sr.)

Matthew & Anna Jones
(Courtesy of Sam Parker, Sr.)

Julian & Christine Hines
(Courtesy of Evalena Hoskins)

John & Katie Habersham and Family
(Courtesy of St. Matthew's Collection)

George Mamie Williams
(Courtesy of the *Savannah Tribune*)

George Williams
(Courtesy of the *Savannah Tribune*)

Dr. & Mrs Fannin Belcher and child
(Courtesy of Ursaline Law)

(Courtesy of Leonard Law, Jr.)

The Priester Family
(Courtesy of Marion Roberts)

Annie Collier & Marie Law
(Courtesy of Leonard Law, Jr.)

Maggie Canty
(Courtesy of Dorothy Canty Bass)

Toney Evans, Benjamin Evans and Lee Evans
(Courtesy of Janie Evans Fowles)

Edward, John & Leonard Law
(Courtesy of Leonard Law, Jr.)

Gussie White
(Courtesy of John White, Sr.)

Bonaparte White
(Courtesy of John White, Sr.)

W. J. & Madline Mitchell, Sr.
(Courtesy of W. J. Mitchell, Jr.)

Mt. Moriah Lodge No. 15 F.& A. M.
(Courtesy of Curtis V. Cooper)

Dr. Simeon Palmer Llyod
(Courtesy of the *Savannah Tribune*)

Dr. Henry M. Collier, Sr.
(Courtesy of John B. Collier)

Dr. Henry M. Collier, Jr.
(Courtesy of the *Savannah Herald*)

Dr. William G. Tyson
(Courtesy the *Savannah Tribune*)

Dr. Clarence Tyson
(Courtesy the *Savannah Tribune*)

Dr. Henry M. Collier, Sr. Office
(Courtesy of John B. Collier)

Dr. Nathaniel H. Collier
(Courtesy of the *Savannah Tribune*)

Dr. Stephen M. McDew, Jr.
(Courtesy of the *Savannah Tribune*)

Dr. Stephen M. McDew, Sr.
(Courtesy of the *Savannah Tribune*)

Dr. J. W. Jamerson 111
(Courtesy of Dr. J.W.Jamerson 111)

Clinic at St. Augustine's Parish Hall
(Courtesy of St. Matthew's Collection)

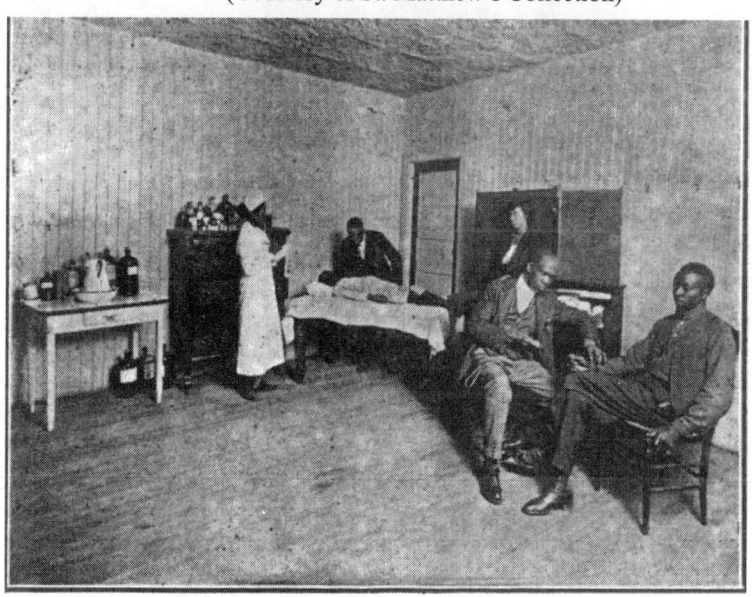

Dunbar Theatre on West Broad Street
(Courtesy of Rose Mary Tyson Matthews)

Monroe Funeral Home, 611 West Broad Street
(Courtesy of the *Savannah Tribune*)

Myrtle Kendrick
(Courtesy of
Carmelita & Altheria Maynard)

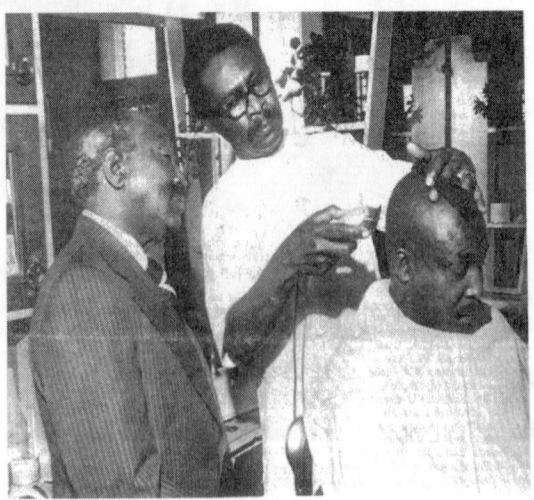

Charlie Johnson and Herbert Stevens
(Courtesy of the *Savannah Morning News*)

Connie Wimberly
(Courtesy the *Savannah Tribune*)

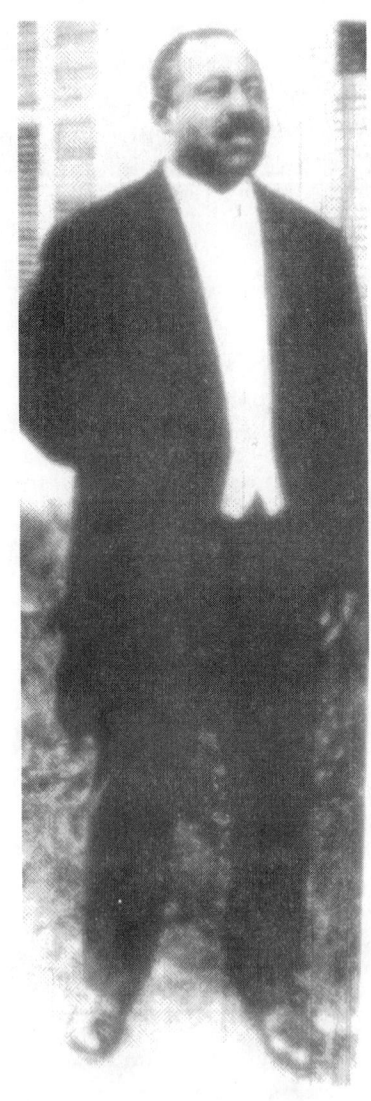

Ross E. Johnson
Headwaiter Pulaski Hotel
(Courtesy of the *Savannah Tribune*)

Savannah-Simmons Mattress Company
318-320 East Bay Street
(Courtesy of the *Savannah Tribune*)

The *Savannah Tribune*
(Courtesy of the *Savannah Tribune*)

Life Member-Bricklayer
(Courtesy of Harry Hunter

Madam Carrie Cargo & Associates
(Courtesy of Louise Williams)

Prof. Robert W. Gadsden
(Courtesy of the *Savannah Tribune*)

Coach Joe Greene
(Courtesy of Beach High School)

Prof. James H. C. Butler
(Courtesy of the *Savannah Tribune*)

Graduation Class 1920
(Courtesy of John Finney)

Teachers: Melinda Smith, Madeline Shrivery and Cornelia McDowell
(Courtesy of the *Savannah Tribune*)

Frances E. Harper Circle
(Courtesy of Lucy G. Solomon & Margie G. Caution)

Students of East Broad Street School
(Courtesy W. J. Mitchell, Jr.)

Alpha Phi Alpha
(Courtesy of Martha Wilson)

Variety Garden Club
(Courtesy of John B. Collier)

The Rev. Ralph Mark Gilbert
(Courtesy of the First African Baptist Collection)

West Broad Street School
(Courtesy of the *Savannah Herald*)

The Ralph Mark Gilbert Civil Rights Museum
(Courtesy of the Museum)

A Brief Chronology of Black Savannah

1526 — Blacks and Spaniards land near Sapelo Sound.

1540 — Hermando de Soto expedition in Georgia.

1716 — Andrew Bryan is born in Goose Creek, South Carolina.

1733-1800

1733 —South Carolinians send several slaves on loan to Oglethorpe and the colonists to clear the land and lay out Savannah.

1734 —Two slaves are jailed in Savannah. Settlers clamor for slaves.

1735 —Trustees officially prohibit slavery in the colony by enacting the "Negro Law" in order to make the colony "more defensible."

1738 — One hundred and twenty-one freeholders petition the Trustees for the right to own slaves, claiming that the colony would fail without slaves. Demand for slaves increases. The Rev. George Whitefield supports the ownership of slaves by the colonists. He uses slave labor on his plantation in South Carolina to subsidize his orphan home at Bethesda.

1739 – The Stono rebellion breaks out in South Carolina. Forty-four blacks and thirty whites killed.

1740 — February 29, a slave is sold at auction in Savannah.

1747 — De facto slavery exists in Savannah as slaves are "practically recognized" in the colony.

1750 —Slavery is officially legalized in Georgia. The black population, by one report, is said to be "349 working Negroes, namely 202 men and 147 women besides children too young for labour." Slaves come mainly from South Carolina and the West Indies. On Saturday July 7, a slave woman is baptized at Christ Church. Several blacks regularly attend services.

1751 — Christ Church operates a school for forty-one slaves. Joseph Ottolenghe becomes headmaster of this school. George Liele is born in Virginia.

1755 — The first comprehensive slave code is promulgated. Andrew Cox Marshall is born in South Carolina.

1758 — The first Affirmative action law passed, permitting the hiring of only white artisans.

1759 — Henry Cunningham is born in McIntosh County.

1762 — Eighty-two slaves entered Savannah and are recorded in the custom house.

1763 — Cemetery for people of color is established. The area eventually encompasses the present location of Rose of Sharon Apartments over to around Jones Street. The exact area is unknown.

1764 — Advertisement: "To be sold on Saturday the 18th at the Watch-house in Savannah, eleven valuable Negroes."

1765 — Slaves establish a maroon site, north of the Savannah River.

1766 — Slaves imported from Africa add their contribution to the culture of the area. Andrew C. Marshall comes to Savannah. Advertisement: "On Tuesday the 25th August will be sold in the town of Savannah Achoice cargo of one hundred slaves, just arrived in the Brigantine ANTELOPE, Thomas Paley Commander, directly from the river Gambia and Sierraleon. By Ingilis and Hall." Five slave ships landed their cargo of slaves.

1767 — The General Assembly orders the building of a lazaretto on a one hundred and four acre lot on Tybee Island about three miles from the lighthouse. There, slaves are kept in quarantine, until they are ready for shipment to Savannah. About forty percent of the slaves entering Savannah come from Africa.

1770 — Slave code prohibits the education of blacks. Slaves are forbidden to assemble together without permission. Advertisement: "For sale on Tuesday the 15th. May, 1770, A cargo consisting of about 200 young and healthy slaves Just arrived, after a short passage, is the ship Cavendish. Captain James Penny, from SierrLeon on the windwardcoast."

1771 — About eight hundred and twenty-one slaves live in Savannah.

1774 — The Rev. John B. Deveaux is born a slave in Savannah.

1775 — Black Anglican Deacon David Margate, attached to Bethesda orphan home, preaches that God would use him to liberate the slaves. He is put on a boat bound for England. Rice becomes the major money crop for Georgia. The Rev. George Liele is ordained a Baptist minister and conducts preaching missions along the Savannah River banks from Augusta to Savannah.

1778 — The British recapture Savannah, aided by black oysterman Quamino Dolly.

1779 — Americans fail to capture Savannah from the British. About 500-800 black Haitians fight with the Americans around the Spring Hill Redoubt. Several local blacks killed. The British "impress" 400 slaves to work on the fortifications, and arm 200 who fight on their side.

1782 — In July, about 3,500 blacks, the exact number is unknown, leave Savannah with the British. The Rev. George Liele goes to Jamaica where he establishes the first Baptist Church on the Island. The Rev. David George goes to Nova Scotia, Canada, and finally to Sierra Leone, in Africa where he establishes Baptist churches. About 300 blacks, some formerly part of the British forces, terrorize plantations on the Savannah River. They call themselves "King of England Soldiers." They are subdued in 1786.

1788 — The Rev. Abraham Marshall, white, and the Rev. Jesse Peter, black, ordain Andrew Bryan who becomes pastor of the Ethiopian Church of Jesus Christ in Savannah.

1789 — Andrew Bryan buys his freedom for fifty pounds sterling.

1790 – The court house on Wright Square, becomes the main venue for selling slaves in Savannah. Brokers display slaves on stands in front of the court house. This commerce lasts from 1790 to 1865.

1793 — Father Andrew Bryan buys a piece of land on Mill Street in Oglethorpe Ward. Eli Whitney "invents" the cotton gin at Mulberry Grove near Savannah. The gin does the work of ten slaves. Congress passes the Fugitive Slave Act.

1795 — Ban on importing slaves from the West Indies. Plot by slaves to revolt discovered by authorities.

1798 – Georgia's new constitution abolishes the slave trade.

1800-1864

1801 — Cotton cultivation increases in uplands. Special Act of legislature required to free slaves.

1802 — Henry Cunningham organizes the present Second African Baptist Church.

1804 — September 8 — storm from 9:00 A.M. to 10:00 P.M., floods Hutchinson Island killing more than one hundred blacks. Rumors of black insurrection rife in Savannah. Book on the Haitian revolution is banned in Savannah.

1806 — Permanent well-organized City Guard established to control slaves.

1808 — U.S. forbids importation of slaves from Africa.

1809 — Savannah has 2,702 whites and 2,640 blacks for a total of 5,342 souls.

1810 — Slaves and free people of color are subject to police control.

1812 — Father Andrew Bryan (1716-1812) dies. He pastored the First Colored Baptist Church for twenty-four years. Free colored men "rendered signal service as a corps of pioneers and in working on the fortifications." He left an estate of $5,000 and a few slaves. William C. Campbell is born a slave in Savannah.

1815 — Father Andrew C. Marshall becomes pastor of the First Colored Church.

1816 — City Council grants lot nineteen in Greene ward to what is now Second African Baptist Church.

1817 — May 28 - The Rev. John B. Deveaux organizes the Old One Hundred Society of Sacred Music.

1818 — Free coloreds must register on entering state and annually. Alexander Harris is born free to free parents. Though at its opening blacks were allowed to attend the Savannah Theater, soon a change in policy dictates that blacks be banned from the entertainment. As one white patron comments on their attendance, "they cannot possibly derive any benefit-and evils will certainly result." Blacks could not legally own real estate nor slaves.

1819 – Black Julien Fromantin, originally from Haiti, opens his underground school to educate free and slave blacks. Economic depression hits Savannah.

1820 — Savannah has 3,866 whites, 582 free coloreds, 3,075 slaves, for a total of 7,523 persons. More than fifty percent of households own slaves. Between the 1820s and 1896 about two hundred local blacks immigrate to Liberia. Yellow fever hits Savannah. Richard Richardson owns nine slaves living in the Owens-Thomas House.

1821— About seventy-five free coloreds formed into the Franklin Fire Engine and Hose Company. Blacks compose the majority of local firemen until the 1870's.

1822 — City Council forbids free people of color being apprenticed to "the trade of carpenter, mason, bricklayer"

1823 — Council stops the public whipping of blacks in market square. Anthony Odingsells owns ten slaves, Prince Cany seven, Maria Cohen six, and Louis Mirault owned six slaves.

1825 — Georgia leads the world in cotton production. Blacks are fifty-three percent of Savannah's population. North Oglethorpe has the largest number of blacks of any ward.

1826 — The Independent Presbyterian Church organizes a Sunday school at First African Baptist Church. James Porter is born a free person of color in Charleston, South Cartolina.

1828 – Blacks attend the Savannah Theater and sit in the side gallery which costs twenty-five cents per seat. One hundred and seventy-eight slaves and ninety-six free people of color work as firemen.

1829 — David Walker's "Appeal to the Colored People of the World" arrives in Savannah. Laws against the education of blacks toughened. Fort Pulaski built, in part, with bricks blacks made at Hermitage Plantation.

1830 — Blacks are forty-five percent of the population. Slave-owning by blacks reaches it highest level.

1831 — City Council grants lot seventy-one in Yamacraw to the First African Baptist Church. The City Council also prohibits blacks being apprenticed to cabinet makers, painters, blacksmiths, tailors, butchers or coopers.

1832 — Schism splits First African Baptist Church into two congregations (present First African Baptist Church, under Marshall with 2,640 members and First Bryan Baptist Church, with 155 members led by Deacon Adam Arguile Johnson). Georgia Infirmary established for the cure of sick African Americans. Thomas F. Williams, a white man, left funds that were used to establish a hospital for blacks. Later, black nurses work in the hospital, but black doctors are barred from practicing in the hospital.

1838 — Trail of Tears, as more than 16,000 Cherokee Indians are expelled from Georgia.

1840 — Savannah has 5,888 whites, 632 free coloreds, 4,694 slaves, for a total of 11,214 persons. About forty-eight percent of households owned slaves. Anyone with a black ancestor in the past three generations is regarded as black. White artisans pay taxes on one hundred slave mechanics. Slaves work for the most prominent builders of Savannah. There are thirty-four black carpenters, seven coopers, two eginers and four ship carpenters in Savannah.

1842 — Born in 1759, the Rev. Henry Cunningham, pastor of the Second African Baptist Church, dies. He pastored the church for forty years.

1845 — The Methodists build Andrew Chapel for black members. State law prohibits blacks from making contracts to erect buildings.

1847 – German sea Captain Hermon Sengstacke buys the slave Tama and marries her.

1848 — Savannah has 7,150 whites, 6,313 blacks for a total population of 13,463 persons. Free people of color live in twenty of the twenty-two wards of Savannah. John H. Deveaux is born in Savannah.

1849— Taxes on slaves are reduced.

1850 — Fugitive slave law enacted. Lumber companies own sixty-five slaves, rice planters seventy-seven and brick makers own twenty-five slaves. River boat companies own 193 slaves. Pulaski Hotel owns sixty-two slaves and the City Hospital also owns slaves. Many "nominal slaves" hire themselves out and pay their owners a set fee. Slaves work on public roads and load boats on the river docks. Savannah has 8,395 whites, 686 free coloreds, 6,231 slaves, for a total of 15,312 persons. Many free blacks work as carpenters, bricklayers, porters, and wagoners. Most of them live in Oglethorpe ward. Anthony Odingsells owns ten slaves, Aspasia Mirault six, Susan Jackson eight, the Rev. Andrew C. Marshall eight and Andrew Morrel owns three slaves. Free coloreds in Chatham County own property valued at $28,850. Blacks are forty-five percent of the population.

1851 — White laborers' opposition to blacks working at skilled trades fails because too many businesses depend on black labor. Advertisement: "$10 Reward. – Runaway from the subscriber on Friday night last, a young Negro woman, named Katy ... She was recently purchased in Charleston, and will probably endeavor to make her way back to that city." Seventeen year old runaway Savannah slave Thomas Simms is arrested in Boston, Massachusetts, and returned to Savannah where he is publicly whipped. Free people of color required to have a white guardian and they could own property if the white guardian held title to the property. One publication states that in Savannah the white man is the "acknowledged superior of the black."

1852 — Laurel Grove Cemetery opens. About fifteen acres are set aside for black burials.

1853 – Advertisement: "For sale — a valuable boy about fourteen years of age, very smart and intelligent, accustomed to wait in the house and capable of tending a horse." Advertisement: "A man about 25 years old, first rate steamboat or mill hand, for sale. Apply to Wm. Wright." Some 400 black firemen on parade are described as the "pick of the colored population, devoted to the protection of the city."

1854 — November 11, the *Savannah Morning News* presses are no longer operated by "relays of the peculiar institution"— slaves, but by the new steam engine. Advertisement: "For sale, a mulatto man, 30 years old-first rate carpenter, also a man, 22 years old, a first rate bricklayer. Apply Wm. Wright." Yellow fever plagues Savannah. Black sea men gain more freedom of movement.

1855 — William Claghorn and others establish St. Stephen's Episcopal Church in the hall of his bakery. Sister Frances, a white nun, operates a school for black children. May 25 – A letter in the *Daily Morning News* suggests that "Uncle" Andrew Marshall be sent up North to "enlighten" Northerners about slavery. The paper considers the suggestion a "complement" to "Uncle Andrew," but is against the idea. Blacks attending the Savannah Theater could buy a special box ticket for fifty cents. The bodies of deceased blacks are exhumed from the black cemetery on the Eastside and reintered in Laurel Grove Cemetery South.

1856 — Born in 1755, Father Andrew Cox Marshall dies. He pastored the congregation for over forty years. Toney, the oldest colored fireman in the city, dies. His funeral was the largest ever seen in the city. More than one thousand Negroes follow the procession. Court House sale: "Negro man sold for $1,355 and a woman for $1,205." These sales indicate not only that "Negroes are commanding good prices," but also that "there is money in our community seeking investment in that species of property." Annual parade of the colored fire companies is reviewed by the mayor and aldermen. The fifty-two free coloreds in the Axmen and Hook and Ladder Company heading the parade of 668 blacks are described by the *Daily Morning News* as "composed of as fine a set of stalwart Negroes as can be found in any city." James Porter, a free person of color, is bought over from Charleston to teach music to St. Stephen's congregation. He soon opens an underground school.

1857 — The U. S. Supreme Court's Dred Scott decision denies blacks U.S. Citizenship. Advertisement: "For hire-a prime carpenter and cabinet maker-apply to David R. Dillon." Advertisement: "For sale. A likely yellow girl, cook, washer, ironer and seamstress, for sale by David R. Dillon, Market Square." Advertisement: "Negroes Wanted. The subscribers wish to hire upon their work on the Augusta and Waynesboro Railroad, a number of prime Negro men. They will pay $15 per month for full hands and all proportion for other rates; wages payable monthly in Savannah. For further information apply at No. 117 Bay Street, Savannah, or of the subscribers at the depot, 79 miles Central Railroad." Advertisement: "The colored class of vocalists who have been for some time under the tuition of Mr. Sturtevant will give a Sacred Concert at St. Andrew's Hall on Friday evening for the benefit of the class. We are told that their instruction in vocal music is such as to display their natural talent to great advantage." Economic panic hits in Savannah.

1858 – Charles Lamar imports slaves in the ship *Wanderer*. A twenty-year old slave of Corine Hutchison, named Sarah, dies in a mishap on the steamer Pulaski. Her owner erects a monument on her grave. Yellow fever hits Savannah. Free blacks pay higher taxes than whites and must work on "public works" for twenty days each year without pay.

1859 — Slaves, men and women, build First African Baptist Church, after working a full day for their owners. The Rev. S. C. G. Daniel, pastor of the First Baptist Church, lays the cornerstone. The members of the First African Baptist Church establish Bethlehem Baptist Church. Slaver Joseph Bryan, on Johnson Square, advertises: "Sale of 440 Negroes. Persons designing to inspect these Negroes will find them at the race course where they can be seen from 10. A. M. to 2 P.M. until day of sale." The 429 slaves, men women and children, from the Pierce Butler estate are sold for more than $300,000. Advertisemnent: "Having bought the negro yard and office of Mr. William Wright, I am fully prepared to receive negroes for sale on commission, or for safe keeping. Joseph Bryan."

1860 —St. Stephen's Episcopal Church buys a former Unitarian Church on Oglethorpe Avenue and moves the building to Troup Square. Savannah has 13,875 whites, 705 free coloreds, 7,712 slaves for a total of 22,292 persons. Some thirty-three percent of households own slaves. Advertisement: "For sale, a likely country raised girl, 17 years old, and a capable servant; also several men, women and children. A. Bryan, Market Square." And, "A number one cook and prime woman with three children. Apply to J. Bryan, Johnson Square." Hundreds of well dressed slaves, with purse in hand, bet various sums on their favorite "nags." Free people of color own $61,800 worth of real estate. Savannah has ten black fire companies. Blacks are thirty-eight percent of the population. The black population more than doubles between 1820 and 1860. There are four white and ten black fire companies in the city. Sixty-eight per cent of the free people of color are mulattos. Black Savannah has twenty-three carpenters, eleven coopers, twenty-one bricklsayers and four blacksmiths. Free colored, Ann Gibbons, owns three slaves and $9,500 worth of real estate.

1861 — Fort Sumter fired on and Georgia secedes. The Rev. Ulysses Houston becomes pastor of First Bryan Baptist Church. Alexander Stephens gives his "cornerstone speech" in Savannah outlining the purpose of the Civil War. Charles Waters is born in Savannah May 19, 1861. His father William Waters was drum-Sergeant in the Republican Blues during the Civil War. Charles Waters became a well-known singer and composer. He composed, *Dark Side of Love, A Mother's Request* and *Suffer the Children*. Master bootmakers agreed not to "employ, hire or learn any Negro the boot-making business."

1862 – General D. Hunter frees slaves at Fort Pulaski and organizes the First South Carolina Volunteer Infantry. Advertisement: "The undersigned will open on the 1st of January next, a mart for the reception and sale at auction of Negro property. J. A. Stevenson."

1863 – A Boat of Negroes attempting to escape to the enemy caught at Proctor's point. Advertisement- "Negroes for sale privately at my mart. 108 Bryan Street. J. A. Stevenson." The colored gallery of the Savannah Theater costs seventy-five cents. President Lincoln signs the Emancipation Proclamation. Fort Pulaski falls to the Union troops.

1864 — December 22, General William T. Sherman enters captured Savannah and sends a Christmas cable to President Lincoln from Savannah.

1865-1899

1865 — Dr. A. T. Augusta head of the Freedman's Hospital is the first black doctor to practice medicine in Savannah. Black leaders meet at First African Baptist Church and organize the Savannah Educational Association. Thursday, January 12, General William Sherman and Secretary of War Edwin Stanton meet with twenty black leaders in the Green-Meldrim House. The Rev. Garrison Frazier defines slavery as, "receiving by irresistible power the work of another man and not by his consent." Four days later General William Sherman issues Special Order #15.

The black Savannah Educational Association operates Bryan Free School in the former Bryan slave mart with James Porter as principal and Oglethorpe Free School in a former Confederate Hospital with Louis B. Toomer principal. Both individuals had operated underground schools during slavery. On February 2, General Saxton, at a meeting in Second African Baptist Church, explains the implications of Sherman's Special Order #15 for blacks. This event gives birth to the "forty acres and a mule" story so firmly held among blacks. The Rev. Ulysses Houston leads a settlement of about 1,000 blacks on Skidaway Island and they have "several hundred acres of land are in advanced state of cultivation." There is a "governor, sheriff and three inspectors on duty on the island, elected by the people and perfect harmony prevails."

Georgia ratifies the fifteenth amendment. Andrew Chapel congregation leaves the white Methodist denomination, and under the influence of the Rev. James Lynch of Maryland and the Rev. C. L. Bradley, of South Carolina, the congregation joins the black African Methodist Episcopal Church, taking the name St. Phillip's A.M.E. The Congress passes the thirteenth Amendment to the U.S. Constitution formally abolishing slavery. Companies C. D. and G. of the 103rd United States Colored Troops leave on the steamer Emelie for Fort Pulaski. Black stevedores strike.

1866 — Vagrancy laws, apprenticeship, convict leasing, farm credit, and other hindrances soon restrict black rights. Congress passes Civil Rights Act. The Rev. James M. Simms organizes the Eureka Lodge, the first Prince Hall Masonic Order in Georgia. The colored schools close their winter session. They are the Yonkers school in the basement of the First African Church; the Hospital School at the hospital east of the park; the Lamar and Andrew schools at Andrew Chapel on New Street; Bethlehem High School at the church, and Bryan School and Oglethorpe School at the Oglethorpe College building. Many blacks participate in drills of the Loyal Leagues outside Savannah. City Council closes Forsyth Park to blacks, but the Federal authorities force a change in policy and blacks are allowed to use the park. Captain John Dillon establishes a chapter of the Ku Klux Klan in Savannah.

1867 — Black Longshoremen strike against the increase of badge fees. The American Missionary Association and the "gobbled-up" black Savannah Educational Association open Beach Institute. James M. Simms publishes the first local black newspaper, the *Southern Radical and Freedmen's Journal*. Several thousand blacks hold a meeting on the commons in the rear of the county jail. Albert Jackson appointed to the Board of Registrars for the city of Savannah. There are 3,061 colored and 2,269 white registered voters. Aaron Burt is arrested for addressing a black meeting in front of the court house. James Porter, James Simms, William Pollard, Ulysses Houston, Simon Mirault are appointed delegates to the Republican convention.

1868 — The Ogeechee rebellion occurs. Federal Troops help quell the uprising but the leader, Charles Thompson, escapes. Blacks take control of the old Fort on Skidaway Island. Blacks vote for the first time. Richard W. White elected clerk of Superior Court. James Porter and James M. Simms elected to represent Chatham County in the Georgia Assembly. Blacks later expelled from the Georgia Legislature. Some blacks are elected coroners. St. Stephen's Episcopal Church members establish the Savannah Benevolent Society, to "relieve the sick and destitute colored people of the city." Blacks hold several public political meetings in Chippewa Square and a riot breaks out. Twenty-five blacks are indicted. The Mayor stops a meeting in the square, but blacks continue the meeting at the First African Baptist Church. St. Philip's A.M.E. Church on New Street is under construction.

1869 — Many blacks, employed, "in find work scheme," to build the Police Headquarters. The First Congregational Church is established at Beach Institute. The Georgia Supreme Court upholds the elction of Richard White as clerk of Superior Court.

1870 —Many blacks migrate to Alabama, Mississippi, Texas, and Arkansas. King Solomon Thomas is appointed a sheriff. Blacks are forty-six percent of Savannah's population.

1871 — The Rev. John H.H. Sengstacke establishes the Woodville Pilgrim Congregational Church outside Savannah. The Governor appoints James M. Simms judge of District Court. White lawyers object. He never serves as a judge. Blacks riot on Louisville Road. St. Paul's C. M. E. Church and Asbury Methodist Churches founded. Dr. Charles H. Taylor has his office at 98 State Street and Dr. Patrick H. Coker has his, at 21 York Street. Coker ran for coroner but lost the election. Eszra Presbyterian is organized.

1872 — The Rev. J. Robert Love, the first black Episcopal rector of St. Stephen's, leaves the church and organizes St. Augustine Episcopal Church in Yamacraw. Blacks stage a successful boycott of horsedrawn segregated street cars. They remain integrated. Democrats take control of city council. The black elite pressures the Board of Education to provide for the education of black children. The board leases St. Stephen's Episcopal Church's private school located in the church's unused rectory, and opens the 220 student school as the first black public school in Savannah's history. Within a few months a mysterious fire damages the building and the public school is transferred to the Scarbrough House on West Broad Street.

James Porter becomes the first principal of this West Broad Street School in the Scarbrough house. He had been a teacher in the school when it was run by the church. The Rev. Henry Turner, pastor of St. Philip's AME on New and Fahm Streets, gives an address to an overflow crowd on the future of the Negro. About 1,000 black rice growers assemble on Bay Street at East Broad Street to protest the contemplated action of the Congress to repeal duty on foreign rice. About four hundred blacks demonstrate at the courthouse. The Chatham Light Infantry and the Forest City Light Infantry is organized. John H. Deveaux, Richard White, L. B. Toomer and A. A. Bradley elected delegates to the Republican convention. The Board of Education fails to take over Beach Institute.

1873 — First Bryan Baptist members are building their church. James Porter elected magistrate in the Fourth District. A. McGilvry elected constable in the Eight District. Lincoln Guards and Chatham Light Infantry, parade in the city. Washington Cornet Band hosts the Chicora Cornet Band from Charleston, South Carolina.

1874 — Benedictine monks arrive to evangelize blacks and establish St. Benedict's Church. The Rev. Henry Turner establishes St. James A.M.E. congregation. John M. Collins, a colored temperance disciple organizes a one hundred member Christian Temperance Association.

1875 — December 4 — John H. Deveaux, Louis B. Toomer, Richard White and Louis Pleasant publish the *Colored Tribune*; later, name changed to the *Savannah Tribune*. Pythagoras lodge with John H. Deveaux as Grand Master is organized. The Rev. Henry Turner addresses the audience. The

Lone Star Cadets is founded. St. Benedict's School on Perry Street is established and one on Isle of Hope.

1876 — The Mutual Benevolent Society is founded with James Porter the first president. The Rev. John H. H. Sengstacke marries Flora Abbott, mother of Robert Abbott. Abbott works on the *Woodville Times* run by the Rev. Sengstacke. The Rev. Edward Brown organizes Mount Zion Baptist Church in Frog Town. Blacks force the removal of signs reading "exclusively for white people" from the court house. The first detachment of Negro soldiers enlisted in Savannah for the colored regiment on the frontier service, leave by the Western and Southern Railroad. The Supreme Court nullifies the black vote. Yellow fever hits Savannah. Blacks and whites swear on separate bibles in the mayor's court.

1877 — All Federal troops withdraw from the South. Abraham Beasley marries Matilda Taylor (later Mother Beasley). He is reported to have been the only black slaver in the city's history.

1878 — First Georgia Battalion (Colored) is organized. Black troops have the first state prize drill. James H. C. Butler is appointed principal of West Broad Street School. Benedictines open a school for blacks on Skidaway Island. The mayor allows black street hucksters to continue practicing their trade. Blacks petition the Savannah Theatre for a "reasonable space be partitioned off" for their use.

1880 — The Colored Debating Society deliberates the topic, "Was Negro slavery of the U.S a curse in its character." The affirmative prevailes. Judge Fleming appoints Abraham Burke a Notary Public. The eighty blacks who struck the Lower Cotton Press are discharged. Baseball tournament of the colored baseball players held at Thunderbolt under the auspices of the National Baseball Association of Savannah. The members of the First Colored Battalion Georgia Volunteers meet at the Lincoln Guards Hall, with Captain J. H. Gardner in the chair and L. B. Toomer is the acting secretary. Blacks are fifty-one percent of Savannah's population.

1881 — Ex-Union soldiers form a Veteran's group with Abram Burke as secretary. The First Georgia Colored Volunteers Battalion under Lieutenant Colonel William A. Woodhouse, have their first parade. The entire colored military including the infantry, artillery and cavalry, uniformed and equipped, gather at the home of John Deveaux, at Habersham and Duffy Streets, and compliment him on being commissioned as a major in the military.

1882 – Women of the Methodist Home Missionary Society open Haven Home School near Burroughs Street.

1883 — A major fire in Yamacraw makes about 1,200 people homeless. Some 600 children are turned away from public schools. William Woodhouse is elected Magistrate in the Fourth District. Some blacks appeal for help to keep the colored cemetery "in good order." Moses Caston, President of the Colored Orphans Home Association, dies in a fire at the warehouse where he worked.

1884 — A petition requesting the appointment of five black policemen is presented to City Council. The Petition is received as information. About seventeen industrious colored men form a syndicate and purchase 200 acres in the Janesville tract, also known as "Old Nicholson place," on White Bluff Road about eleven miles from Savannah. They raise corn and potatoes during the summer and fish during the winter.

1885 – Jane Deveaux dies. Her tomb inscription states: "Sacred to the memory of Jane A. Deveaux Died June 12 A.D. 1885 Aged 74 years 10 months 29 days A devoted Christian celebrated as an early educator of her people she has built for herself a name more enduring than monuments of stone or brass."

1886 — About five thousand to eight thousand blacks gather on the banks of the Ogeechee River to witness the Rev. Ulysses Houston, pastor of the First Bryan Baptist Church, baptize one hundred and thirty-eight new members. An earthquake shakes Savannah. Dr. Patrick H. Coker dies. He is one of the first black doctors to practice in Savannah. Sacred Heart parish founded for blacks changes to a white congregation.

1887 — Mother Beasley establishes St. Francis Colored Orphan Home at East Broad and Gaston Streets. Cyrus Campfield, jeweler, formerly with S. P. Hamilton, opens his own business at 11 Whitaker Street. King Solomon Thomas dies. He was elected magistrate of the Fourth District G. M. in 1868, and served four years. Longshoremen strike for an increase in wages. State legislature passes the Glen Bill banning black and white children studying in the same school. Three white boys arrested and fined for disturbing worship at St. Stephen's Episcopal Church on Troup Square.

1888 — November 28, some residents riot in Yamacraw. One black is killed. Eight colored nurses leave for Jacksonville to care for yellow fever victims. A group raises $800 at the fair for First African Baptist Church's tower bell. City grants permission for the First African Baptist Church to add twenty-six feet to the building. Black Baptists celebrate a century of Baptist worship. The Reverends E. K. Love and James M. Simms write books supporting the primacy of First African Baptist Church and First Bryan Baptist Church respectively.

1889 — The cornerstone of St. Benedict's church is laid. The Rev. Ulysses Houston dies. His funeral reported to be the largest ever in the city's history. Between 3,000 to 8,000 persons attend the service. He was pastor of the First Bryan Baptist Church for twenty-eight years, and was regarded as, "one of the oldest and one of the most notable of the Southern colored ministry." A black Basketball League is organized. Savannahian James R. Porter, the son of the Rev. James Porter, graduates from Dental School. Sol C. Johnson becomes editor of the *Savannah Tribune* as John H. Deveaux is appointed collector of customs for the port of Brunswick.

1890 — Masons lay the cornerstone of St. James A.M.E. Church and Nicolsonboro Baptist Church. Blacks are fifty-three percent of the city's population. West Indian born, the Rev. Alexander Ellis, organizes Beth Eden Baptist Church on December 28, 1891, with 400 members in the Duffy Street Hall. Regular services are held in the Mozart Hall at St. Julian Street near the *Savannah Tribune* office.

1891 — The Savannah Negro Laborers Union strike to protest reduction in pay. The first segregation Act separates blacks and whites in state. Attempt made to organize a home for poor blacks. Father William Gray organizes St. John's Baptist Church. The Rev. J. F. Gillens organizes Gaines A.M.E. Church. Virginia born John H. Kinckle becomes the first black licensed to practice law in Savannah. Dr. Brunner, the city's health officer, regards Laurel Grocve Cemetery South as "a disgrace to the city."

Blacks organize the Workingman's Loan and Building Association which obtains a charter. Attempt made to burn Bethel A.M.E. Church. The black Methodists purchase a lot and building of Morris Mission on Roberts Street. The Waiters Grand Union celebrates its fourteenth anniversary with a parade and banquet. Georgia State Industrial College, now Savannah State University, founded with Richard R. Wright as its first president. Dr. A. T. Augusta, the first black doctor to practice in Savannah, dies in Washington. Cyrus Campfield, well-known jeweler, dies. Beth Eden Baptist Church buys the lot facing Lincoln Street for their new church. St. Thomas A.M.E. Church is dedicated.

1892 — The Peoples Saving and Loan Institute is organized with J. W. Searle as president. The Chatham baseball club wins two of the three games with the Fearnots of Charleston. Prof. Samuel Morse's forty voice Savannah Choral Association makes its initial bow at Beach Auditorium. Drs. T. James Davis, S. C. Snelson, C. Bryant Whaley, and Cornelius McKane organize the Southern Medical Association. Members unveil monument over the grave of the Rev. U. Houston. The *Savannah Tribune* reports that almost 1,000 black children are unable to find school accommodation. An attempt is made to begin a home for the poor. Anthony Desverney dies. He was born in Charleston, South Carolina, in 1831, came to Savannah in 1866, and was a cotton shipper.

The City and Suburban Railroad discharges all black drivers and hires white ones. The black Forest City Shoe company opens at Whitaker and York Streets. Colored citizens celebrate Emancipation Day with a parade. Major W. H. Royall commands the colored troops and Col. William Woodhouse is grand Marshall of the parade. Black laundry women strike the Troy steam laundry at Bay and Lumbar Streets because the new owner hired only white women. An attempt is made to discharge S. S. McFall as keeper of the colored cemetery. Blacks protest against Dr. Hennessey, the city physician who refused to attend to Ed. Tolbert, a black man who was seriously cut, unless he paid for the treatment. The Rev. Richard Bright of St. Stephen's Episcopal Church opens a kindergarten and elementary school near the church.

1893 — Dr. Alice Woodby McKane assisted by her husband Dr. Cornelius McKane, establishes the McKane Training School for Nurses. A hurricane topples the one hundred foot steeple of First African Baptist Church and the steeple of St. Phillip A.M.E. Teacher's Aid Society organized at West Broad Street School. John F. Andrews, a black man, is elected magistrate by the Seventh District. The Carpenters Union # 688 chartered with William Woodhouse president. The Gothic style Beth Eden Baptist Church designed by architect Henry Urban is built on Lincoln Street between Wayne and Gordon Streets. The facility is expected to cost about $25,000. Parents protest the decision of the Board of Education to force the children to return to the fire damaged East Broad Street School. Some 800 children are out of school due to lack of space. Judge George A. Davison dies. He was elected magistrate of the Fifth G. M. district in 1889 and was connected the the *Weekly Echo*. Davison organized the Georgia Cadets, a junior company, and Sergeant Major of the First Battalion.

The Rev. Frank Keating dies. He sang at the funeral of Mayor Wayne "for which he received the commendation of the entire city." Drs. J. H. Bugg and S. C. Snelson open a colored drug store at Liberty Street near East Broad Street. The black elite gathers to welcome Dr. S. Palmer Lloyd, the first Savannah black person to become a doctor and return home to practice medicine. The Rev. Alexander Harris organizes Mount Tabor Baptist Church. Two blacks, Lewis and Edwards, open a tailoring establishment on Broughton Street near West Broad Street. The First African Baptist Church of Bolton Street is established. The *Savannah Tribune* reported:

> Savannah has several colored men in business whom the race may well feel proud of. Among them is Maj. W. H. Royall, who conducts an undertaking establishment second to none in the city. His place is stocked with the finest teams in the city. There can also be named Capt. F. F. Jones who has one of the largest butchering stalls in the market; Mr. J. B. Sheftall, the green grocer, who is a large real estate owner; Mr. I. M. Dowse, another green grocer; Mr. J. D. Lloyd the East Broad Street grocer, and many others, who are doing well in their respective lines.

1894 — The Masons lay the cornerstone of Bethel A.M.E. Eugene Browning and John H. Toomer organize the *Savannah Journal*. Evangelical ministers organize. The *Savannah Tribune* calls for the appointment of black policemen in the city. On March 17, The *Savannah Tribune* reproduces a report from the *Mercantile Review,* a local publication:

> Last but by no means least, is our old friend Sheftall, the whole-souled butcher who is located at the corner of New Houston and Abercorn Streets. It is now forty-five years since Sheftall opened up to sell steaks, chops, and cutlets to the public,

and during all these years fraught with war and financial troubles, he has steered his way clear and ever paid dollar for dollar, a record of which any man should feel proud. He has gotten rich, too; owns several pieces of property; was born and raised in Savannah, and Savannah with him is the first place in the world. His stock is complete with native and western meats and a side line is made of market produce. We wish him continued success, as he deserves it. (*Savannah Tribune*, March 17, 1894.)

1895 — In March, the Steamship *Hausa* sails for Liberia with 202 emigrants — some from Savannah. Dr. Simeon Palmer Lloyd is appointed first black city physician. The Rev. J. W Roberts opens private school in Ezra Presbyterian Church on West Broad Street. Gussie Freeman Burton, Emma Collier and A. E. Randolph are the first graduates of the McKane Training School for Nurses. Many blacks duped by a white man in charge of migration to Liberia. All black ministers in the city preach on the "iniquity of policy playing." They claim that the habit is "doing more to ruin a certain class of our people than mostly any other habit."

Col. John H. Deveaux commands the First Battalion Georgia Troops, Colored, in the Emancipation Day parade. Captain J. F. Jones commands the Savannah Hussars, and Captain J. C. Simmons the Artillery. The Rev. L. B. Maxwell, pastor, celebrates the first service in the newly built First Congregational Church. College Park Baptist Church organized. Col. William H. Woodhouse and S. P. Miller open a carpenter shop at 71 President Street. Mrs. E. L. Harding operates a lodging house at 50½ Reynolds Street near Wheaton Street. The Rev. James Porter dies. He was born in Charleston, South Carolina, in 1826. He operated an underground school in Savannah and was elected to the Georgia house from Chatham County.

1896 — St. Paul's C.M.E. Church at Russell and Maple Streets holds a rally to raise funds to complete the church. The Drs. McKane return to Savannah and establish the McKane Hospital for Women and Children and Training School for Nurses at Thirty-sixth and Florence Streets. Ezra Presbyterian Church is destroyed by a hurricane. This hurricane also destroys St. Phillip's A.M.E. Church. The congregation splits into three parts. The U. S. Supreme Court in *Plessy v.Ferguson* upholds the constitutionality of "separate but equal" facilities.

The Steamship *Laurada* leaves for Liberia with 311blacks. The Mechanics Investment Company is organized. Charles Coleman, colored, drives "Old Socks" to victory at the Doyles race course in Thunderbolt. The Board of Education buys the hall of the Workingmen Union Association for use as a black school. Several white men board the West End car and harass black passengers. Someone shoots Stephen Gibbons who dies some days later. The Grand Jury recommends that West Broad Street School be closed and replaced by a new one. Mrs. F. A. M. Mirault runs a river front resort at Thunderbolt.

1897 — Dr. William Pollard, a veterinary surgeon dies. He was born in Savannah in 1824, and educated in one of the black underground schools. Years later he graduated from Ohio State University. The *Savannah Morning News* reports that Pollard was a surgeon "of great skill and made an enviable reputation in that capacity." St. Philip's A.M.E. members buy a white Methodist church on Charles and West Broad Streets. Services are held at Duffy Street Hall. Ezra Presbyterian members sell the property on West Broad and buy another piece of property on Oglethorpe Avenue and Randolph Street. Asbury Church plans to build a new edifice. A Young Men's Christian League organized at First Congregational Church. St. Paul's C.M.E. Church at Maple and Russell Streets is dedicated. The Rev. W. A. Dinkins is the pastor. Cornerstone of Beth Eden Baptist Church laid. Dr. F. D. Lambert has his dental office at 534 East Oglethorpe Avenue.

1898 — John H. Deveaux is appointed collector of customs for the port of Savannah. Attorneys John B. Kinckle and Abraham Tucker form the first black law firm at 110 West Bryan Street. Several colored plumbers organize the Merchants Plumbing Company at 38 Montgomery Street. C. P. Davis is elected president; G. W. Williams, vice-president, John M. Roston, secretary, and E. B. Knight, general manager. Captain Joseph Mirault dies. He commanded the Forest City Light Infantry and was a letter carrier. Mother Beasley's community of nuns is surpressed.

After 1900

1900 — Wage Earners Bank founded with $102. Jim Crow is King. Blacks are fifty-one percent of the city's population.

1901 – Albert Jackson dies. He was born in Savannah in 1842 and was educated in one of the black underground schools and at Harvard Institute in Boston, Massachusetts. He was the first President of the Wage Earners Bank located at 22 State Street.

1902 — Col. George Mercer, President of the Board of Education, warns that should blacks be allowed to use the proposed public library, the books would soon be found in the pawn shop. City Council votes to give Charity Hospital twenty-five dollars per month. The legislature restores the rank of Lieutenant Col. to John H. Deveaux commander of the First Battalion Infantry, Georgia State Troops Colored. Captain Louis M. Pleasant dies.

1903 —Mother Beasley dies. She conducted an underground school during slavery. In 1869, she married Abraham Beasley and after his death in 1877, she entered the religious life. Beasley donated most of her wealth to the Catholic Church. Forty-five business men meet in the *Savannah Tribune* office and organize the Negro Business League. Attorney A. L. Tucker is elected president, Clarence F. Jones, vice-president, S. M. Jackson, secretary, and Sol Johnson, treasurer. Walter S. Scott opens his dry goods store, gent's furnishings and notions store at 120 State Street near Barnard Street. Dr.

T. Janmes Davis dies. He was born in the West Indies but was one of the first black doctors to practice in Savannah. He was active in many Savannah organizations.

1904 — Prof. Robert W. Gadsden is appointed principal of East Broad Street School. Walter S. Scott moved his dry goods business from State Street to 462 West Broad Street. Louis B. Toomer dies. Born in Charleston, South Carolina, he came to Savannah in his youth and was one of the founders of St. Stephen's Episcopal Church. Toomer ran an underground school during slavery. Prof. J. C. Ross, a black Canadian, dies. He was principal of East Broad Street School. Thos T. Harden dies. In 1881, he published the *Savannah Weekly Echo*.

1905 — The Savannah Men's Sunday Club is founded with Monroe Work as the first president. This protest group exists until about 1911. The state of Georgia disbands the Colored militia. Major William H. Royall dies. His funeral home, now Bynes Royall, is the oldest black business in present day Savannah. Jackson B. Sheftall dies. He was born in Savannah in 1836 and was a mulatto butcher and "highly regarded in business circles as well as in social circles." Dr. J. W. Jamerson lands in Savannah and begins his practice of dentistry.

1906 — Attorney Abraham Tucker, and other leading blacks, organize the Savannah Library Association which opens a library on Hartridge Street. Atlanta experiences race riots. Blacks boycott Savannah street cars. This attempt fails. Daniel Simons operates his mattress company at 318-320 Bay Street. Whittier H. Wright who worked on the *Philadelphia Colored Directory* publishes a *Directory of Colored Business and Professional Men in Savannah*. Some one hundred and forty businesses are listed. Miss A. Pearl Thompson is licensed as the first black pharmacist in Savannah. She graduated from Meharry Medical College.

1907 – A *Savannah Tribune* editorial advises readers "Do not patronize Jim Crow bar rooms. Our women should not make purchases from grocery stores having Jim Crow departments. Don't be Jim Crowed." The Society of African Missions of Lyons takes over the ministry to black Catholics.

1908 — Georgia disenfranchises blacks. The *Savannah Tribune* moves to 462 West Broad Street. The convict-lease system abolished. Ezra Presbyterian Church buys a building on East Broad Street at McDonough and Perry Streets.

1909 — The Rev. Alexander Harris, John H. Deveaux, Prof. Samuel Morse and Dr. Simeon Palmer Lloyd die. The Franciscan sisters convent at Gaston and East Broad Streets is dedicated. The nuns teach at St. Benedict's School. The Rev. Richard Bright, rector of St. Stephen's Episcopal Church, is appointed Archdeacon for colored work in the Diocese of Georgia. Blacks and whites segregated in prisons.

1910 — A colored branch of the YMCA is organized with C. C. Miller president. Butler Presbyterian Church is dedicated. Blacks are fifty-one percent of city's population. Col. William H. Woodhouse dies. He was "among the last of that class of old citizens that have been so prominent in affairs in this community." Father Ignatius Lissner organizes St. Anthony in Springfield Terrace.

1912 —The Rev. James M. Simms dies. The Rev. Nathaniel McPherson Clarke is called as pastor of Beth Eden Baptist Church. The *Savannah Tribune* strongly opposes the growing custom of Sunday funerals and claims "we do not know of any people, save ours, who are so much given to unnecessarily elaborate funeral displays." Mt. Zion Baptist Church at West Broad and Minis Streets buys First Bryan Baptist Church at West Broad Street and Waldburg Lane for $9,500. The church seats 300 persons. The Georgia Infirmary at Abercorn and Thirty-fifth Streets buys property at Florence and Lavinia Streets near Charity Hospital. The laundry drivers meet at the home of E. T. Smalls and organize the laundry drivers association. Dr. Cornelius McKane dies. He assisted his wife in the establishment of the McKane Training School for Nurses in 1893. The Seventh Day Adventists establish a mission in Savannah.

1913 — Prof. Robert W. Gadsden conducts the first public singing of *Lift Every Voice and Sing* in Savannah, in the presence of James Weldon Johnston. Pekin Theater opens. Prof. J. G. Lemon passes the Georgia bar and is admitted to practice. Savannah native Dr. Ferebee, graduates from Howard University and passes the Georgia Dental Board. He opens his office at 603 Gwinnett Street. The Urban League is established. Madame C. J. Walker of Indiana noted teacher of hair culture among black women, visits Savannah and stays at the home of Mrs. M. E. Tolbert at 506 Hartridge Street. The Rev. Junius L. Taylor, rector of St. Stephen's Episcopal Church organizes the Men's Club "to help the young men of the church and the city along all lines." Local railway mail clerks organize a branch of the National Association of Colored Railway Postal Clerks. E. W. Sherman is elected president.

1914 – The Wage Earners Loan and Investment Company builds a new bank at West Broad and Alice Streets for $40,000. Carnegie Library is built on Henry Street opposite Dixon Park, a black middle class neighborhood. Chatham Cycle Club holds Labor Day road races. Frank Smith wins by doing fifty-nine miles in sixty-one minutes. Drs. Fonvielle and Moody buy the Savannah Pharmacy from Lee Chemical of Albany. The Board of Education builds Cuyler Street School, the first public school built for blacks. The A. M. E. Church builds Central Park Normal and Industrial Institute on White Bluff Road and St. Philip's A. M. E. Church on West Broad and Charles Streets for $35,000.

1915 —The boll weevil appears in Georgia. State examiners close thirty-five black barber shops. First Congregational Church opens a free kindergarten. Savannah Savings and Real Estate Corporation, capitalized at $100,000 opens at 468 West Broad Street. Edward Desverney dies. He was a wealthy cotton broker.

1916 —Hundreds gather at the Rail Station and police arrest 200 blacks as they attempt to leave for work in the North. James H. C. Butler of the *Savannah Tribune* is charged with exporting black labor. This perhaps triggers the black exodus to the North. A monument to the Rev. George Liele is erected in front of First Bryan Baptist Church. The Urban League opens a playground for children. Chatham Mutual Life and Health Insurance Company is organized with A. H. Dunbar as president and Duncan Pringle as secretary.

Frank A. Dilworth Sr., opens a shoe shop at 43 Barnard Street. Fleming Tucker cashier at the Mechanics bank, is licensed to practice law in Georgia. Madam C. J. Walker again visits Savannah. Double sessions begin in black public schools. St. Benedict's new school and rectory is dedicated. Prof. James Middleton dies. He was "one of the oldest and most efficient musicians Savannah has ever produced." About 1891, he founded the Union Cornet Band. Isaac Butler dies. He was born in Savannah in 1830 and was a foreman of the Tomichichi Fire Company No. 7. He left an estate valued at about $32,000.

1917 —James W. Johnson organizes a local branch of the NAACP in the Savannah Home Association with Dr. Belcher as its first president. The branch has sixty members and attorney J. G. Lemon is the secretary/treasurer. The United States enters W.W. I. A local tennis club defeats a Charleston team. A Catholic religious order of black nuns is organized. Black women organize the Toussaint L'Ouverture colored branch of the American Red Cross. The NAACP and others protest moving houses of prostitution to the Westside. A colored man in dying condition is refused admission to the Savannah Hospital. Frank Callen appointed juvenile probation officer. Fire damages Meldrim Auditorium at the Georgia State College. Five Negroes are convicted in police court for disorderly conduct. They distributed poems to the public which "may incite a riot among the colored people of the city, as well as over Georgia."

1918 — The Peking Theater is gutted by fire. Georgia leads nation in lynching from 1889 to 1918. The Savannah Federation of Colored Women's Clubs is established. The Federation opens Chatham Protective Home for girls at Thunderbolt. J. Gordon Dingle passes local bar examination. He had been trained at Howard University. Monroe funeral home added Studebaker service wagon. Business men leave for St. Louis to attend the National Businessmen League convention. Four hundred Longshoremen go on strike over back pay. Attorney F. B. Pettie and E. W. Sherman publish the *Savannah Journal*. Prof. John McIntosh, principal of Maple Street School dies. He was elected to the Georgia house from Liberty County in 1880. Rosa Lula Barnes dies in New York. She was born in Alabama but became a prominent business woman and lodge personality in Savannah. She built her home in the 500 block of West Henry Street.

Railroads employ colored women to pickup scrap iron. Upon being forced to lift cross tires and shovel dirt, they quit. Father J. Henry Brown becomes vicar of St. Augustine's Episcopal Church. City Council refuses the request of white drivers who want colored drivers removed to the north end of the Union Station. The Toussaint L'Ouverture branch of the American Red Cross serves 400 black soldiers passing through the city. The Urban League operates a kindergarten in Yamacraw. The colored people of Chatham County contribute $200,000 to War Savings on Pledge Day. Four hundred longshoremen strike for back pay.

1919 — Private James Williams is awarded the French "Croix de Guerre" medal for bravery in battle. William McKelvey opens a tire repair shop at West Broad and Gordon Streets. Twenty-five business men leave on the "Gold Coast Special" coach for St. Louis, Missouri. Lucius Williams is elected vice-president of the National Business League. Edward Perry establishes the Liberty Mutual Life and Health Insurance Company at 721 West Broad Street.

Mrs Quarterman, Mrs. Candis and Mrs. Adel Hemby pass the embalmers board examination. Weldon Lodge petitions for incorporation. Father J. Henry Brown is appointed Archdeacon in charge of Negro work in the Episcopal Diocese of Georgia. The Savannah Pharmacy opens its third store at Randolph Street and Oglethorpe Avenue. Over 1,200 returning soldiers receive a rousing reception from thousands as a big parade is staged. The parade is regarded as "the grandest and most dignified demonstration ever held in this city by Negroes." The American Missionary Association closes Beach Institute. Eureka Aid and Athletic Club founded in 1888, buys a club house.

1920 — The Wage Earners Bank is the first black bank in the county to cross one million dollars in assets. West Indian born J. W. Johnson opens new photo studio at 819 West Broad Street, near Bolton Street. Captain Edward Seabrook dies. He operated a funeral home for many years. Edward Wicks dies. He was born in Savannah in 1842, served in the Union army, was an adjutant in the Robert Shaw Post of the Grand Army, and was a deacon of First Bryan Church for fifty years. Blacks are over forty-seven percent of City's population. Dr. J. H. Bugg dies.

1921— The Dunbar Theater is the only fireproof theater in the city. It is steam heated and well ventilated. Prof. James H. C. Butler dies. He was the principal of West Broad Street School from 1878 to his death. Miss Alice Miller dies. Both taught at West Broad Street School for a combined total of ninety-six years.

1922 — Chatham/Savannah Tuberculosis clinic for colored sufferers opens in St. Augustine's Parish Hall. Some 146 homes are visited and 434 persons seen in the clinic. The Waldorf Social-Civic Club is established. City Council passes and ordinance banning "jitter-bugging" or jazz music in the city under a fine of one hundred dollars. The Savannah Federation of Colored Women's Clubs establishes a medical, dental and surgical free clinic for children in Cuyler Street School. White and black doctors volunteer their services free of charge. Colored auto races held on Labor Day at the fair ground. The Federation establishes a home for wayward girls in Thunderbolt across from the Georgia State Industrial College. Blacks mark Armistice Day with automobile and three horse races at the Tri-State Exposition track. Joe Bruen, the first black to win a dirt track championship, regains his supremacy in a Chambers special.

1924 — Royall Undertaking's new home located at West Broad and Gaston. National Council of Colored Workers in the Episcopal Church meets at St. Augustine's. Bishop Grace baptizes 300 persons, with thousands in attendance. The Wolves Club is established at Young's Café on West Broad Street.

1926 – Daniel Simmons dies. He operated the Simmons Mattress company for many years.

1927 — Decree issued stating that having a black ancestor makes one black.

1928 – Wage Earners Bank placed in the hands of the state examiners. According to the *Savannah Tribune* "constant withdrawals of deposits" was the immediate cause of the collapse. The *Savannah Tribune's* editorial after the fall, regards the collapse of the bank as a great disaster, but emphatically states, "we must carry on."

1929 – The Board of Education builds a second school for blacks, Florence Street School. Lucius E. Williams dies. He came to Savannah in 1895 and was a railway mailman. Later he served as president of the Wage Earners Bank.

1930 —N. A. Branham, and several others, meet in McKelvey-Powell Hall to organize a branch of the NAACP. Donald Thomas, a glazier, is elected President, with N. A. Branham as vice-president, Samuel A. Brown, as secretary, and the Rev. John Q. Adams, as treasurer. Dr. William Blackman dies. A Guyanese by birth, he was attached to Charity hospital from 1895 when he served as superintendent. Attorney Foster B. Pettie dies. He practiced in Savannah for some twenty-five years. Blacks are forty-five percent of the city's population.

1931 — Bishop Grace baptizes more than 700 persons and his church purchases seventeen acres on West Victory Drive.

1932 —Father Gustave H. Caution, Marion O. Johnston, John Delaware, S.L. White Sr., Prof. Robert W. Gadsden, Duncan Scott, and Frank Callen establish colored boys scout troops in Savannah. About 800 persons gather at court house in support of Bishop Grace.

1933 – Nurse Alethia Saulter dies. She was head nurse at Charity hospital and did additional study at Harlem Hospital in New York City.

1934 – Duncan Scott dies. He and his brother, Walter Scott, operated many businesses in Savannah. Prof. Kermit O. Smalls of the Georgia State Industrial College for Colored Youth publishes the *Year Book of Colored Savannah*.

1935 —Mack Branham retires after forty-four years as a mailman. Mrs. Mamie George Williams dies. She was a very prominent Republican Committee woman and a social activist. Mrs. Sarah Flemister Butler dies. "Miss Sara," as she was called, taught with her husband at West Broad Street School for more than fifty years. The *Savannah Tribune's* editor Sol. C. Johnson, one of her former students, reported: "No teacher was more beloved than Mrs. Butler, and not any of them surpassed her in encouraging higher education." The Rev. Samuel T. Redd dies. He served as pastor of Butler Prtesbyterian Church from 1904 to 1933.

1936 — Black leaders pressure the Work Projects Administration authorities for their fair share of benefits. Dr. Neslie W. Este dies. He was born in the West Indies and graduated from Meharry Medical College. Dr. Este practiced here for thirty-two years.

1938 — Savannah has twenty-five black physicians, six dentists, four lawyers, and almost two million dollars in real property. The free clinic moved to the basement of Charity hospital. Albert P. Grant dies. He operated a tonsorial parlor, for a white clientele, on Broughton Street for forty years and left an estate "estimated to be slightly over $20,000." Contractor James Welch dies. He was regarded as "one of the best known building contractors in the city."

1939 – Governor Leverett Sattonstall of Massachusetts appoints Savannah born First Lieutenant Cornelius McKane, son of Doctors Cornelius and Alice McKane, as his personal aid. Contractor W. B. Brown dies. He built "some of the leading buildings on West Broad Street and many of the better class of homes throughout the city."

1940 — Prof. Asa Gordon takes over the editorship and management of the *Savannah Journal*. Robert Abbott dies. He grew up in Savannah and later, in 1906, started the *Chicago Defender*, the first black daily newspaper in the country. Father J. Henry Brown, former vicar of St. Augustine's Episcopal Church, and Archdeacon for colored work in the Diocese, dies. Blacks are forty-five percent of city's population.

1941 — Professor Asa Gordon is fired from Savannah State College because he published articles critical of Jim Crow. The Rev. Ralph Mark Gilbert reinvigorates the NAACP branch founded in 1917, and registers 147 new members. Lachlan M. Pollard dies. He was a mail carrier, a funeral home manager, and a Vestryman of St. Stephen's Episcopal Church for many years. Mrs. Josephine Stiles Jennings dies. She was regarded as "one of the most active Negro business women" in the city. The Rev. Richard Bright, former rector of St. Stephen's Episcopal Church, dies. Nurse Lula Brown Johnson dies. She was one of the first graduates of the Mckane Training School for Nurses. She practiced private nursing for more than twenty years and was "highly esteemed and respected by members of both races."

1942 – Dr. Walter Moody dies. He came to Savannah in 1910 and four years later, with Dr. Fonvielle, started the Savannah Pharmacy.

1943 – The local NAACP chapter has 2,323 adult members and 609 youth council members.

1944 — Abolition of the poll-tax. The Supreme Court prohibits the white-only primary. Blacks now have power to influence the vote.

1945 – The Episcopal Diocese of Georgia votes to change its constitution to allow representation of black clergy and laity in its convention. Blacks had been thrown out of the convention around the same time that blacks were disenfranchised in Georgia.

A black woman boards a bus on West Broad Street and sits beside a white man. After she gets off the bus at Lincoln Inn a fracas breaks out and shots are fired. The bus conductor shoots James Braxton, twenty-five years, in his leg. He is treated at the Georgia Infirmary. A nearly twenty-three acre site on Hopkins Street between Forty-Fifth and Forty-Eighth Streets proposed for new black high school. Federal Judge T. H. Davis rules that blacks are entitled to vote in the white primaries.

1946 — The Hub, a black business and professional civic organization, the Longshoremen, and the NAACP register over 19,000 black voters. Some 3,000 colored World War II veterans meet at the YMCA under the temporary chairmanship of Major T. J. Hopkins, to organize themselves as the Negro Veterans of All Wars. This group pledges to work for better schools, housing and street lighting. Monsignor T. J. McNamara calls Negro disfranchisement "un-American." Greyhound drivers reminded to maintain Georgia law on the segregation of passengers when they arrive in the state.

1947 — The Rev. Ralph Mark Gilbert and others pressure Mayor John Kennedy to appoint the first nine black policemen in the state of Georgia. The original nine officers are sworn in Saturday, May 3, 1947, in the presence of the Rev. Ralph Mark Gilbert, pastor of the First African Baptist Church, John W. McGlockton, President of the Citizens Democratic Club, and many others. John White, Milton Hall, Leroy Wilson, Howard Davis, William Malone, Frank Mullino, Alexander Grant, Stepney Houston, and James Nealy, are the first officers. The authorities expect black police men to "clean up gambling and vice in all colored sections." Chatham County had Negro deputies for some twenty-five years. A colored recreation center and swimming pool opens at Ogeechee Road near Fortieth Street.

Dr. Mary McLeod Bethune, President of Cookman College, Daytona Beach, Florida, is the principal speaker at the Emancipation Day celebration at St. Philip's A.M.E. Church. Cyrus A. Wright of the NAACP Youth Council read the emancipation proclamation. Wilton S. Scott, chairman of the education committee of the Hub writes the Board of Education citing eighteen needs of black schools. The group wants a high school and a Negro Assistant Superintendent. The West Broad Street YMCA launches a drive to raise $10,000 to extend the work of the organization. Three additional black policemen are added to the department.

1949 – The newly built St. Benedict's Catholic Church at East Broad and Gaston Streets is dedicated.

1950 — Westley W. Law becomes the president of the local NAACP branch and later begins weekly mass meetings. Mount Zion Church on West Broad Street is rededicated. The building was recently brick veneered and two new rest rooms were added. Captain John Starr dies. He obtained his pilot license for steam vessels in 1902. Blacks are forty percent of the city's population. Dr. P. M. Sessoms dies.

1951 – The Hub claims that ninety new classrooms are needed in black schools. White Board of Education member, Captain F. W. Spencer citing inequality in the system, requests four new black schools. Emma Quinney dies. She was the first principal of Florence Street School. Contractor William Judson Ayers dies. He built the Rosa Barnes house at 525 East Henry Street, his own home at 539 East Henry Street, and Dr. Henry Collier's home on Thirty-Seventh Street.

1952 — Only three of the sixteen black schools are accredited. Catholics plan to build new Catholic high school for Negroes. Blacks petition to use part of white beach at Tybee. A committee lays Greenbriar's cornerstone. Governor Talmadge promises to answer U. S. Supreme Court ruling on segregation by closing all the schools. Longtime waiter at the Hilton Hotel, J. A. Walker dies. He had served three Presidents at the facility. Mrs. Eliza Pollard Deveaux, "Miss Sis," dies. She taught at St. Stephen's Episcopal Church school and then at West Broad Street School for more than fifty years.

1953 — Blacks request that one of their own be appointed to the Board of Education. NAACP request that no more white schools be built until the number of white pupils in double sessions equals that of black children. The Board of Education rules out double sessions for white children but double sessions continue for black children. The school system has 17,612 white children and 10,396 black children for a total of 26,008 children. Attorney James G. Lemon dies. He practiced law in Savannah for nearly thirty years.

1954 – The Supreme Court issues the *Brown v. Board of Education* ruling. Sol C. Johnson owner and editor of the *Savannah Tribune* dies. He had been editor for sixty-five years. Dr. J. Earl Fonvielle dies. Mrs. Mary Moody dies. She was the wife of Dr. Walter Moody one of the founders of the Savannah Pharmacy. Dr. Nathaniel Collier dies. He practiced dentistry for some thirty years.

1955 – The NAACP threatens court action over teacher firings proposed by the Board of Education. The State drops its edict against black teachers who belong to the NAACP. The local chapter of the NAACP petitions the Board of Education to integrate black and white schools. Longshoremen strike. Dr. Stephen McDew, Sr., dies. He came to Savannah in 1923 and practiced here for thirty-two years. Frank Dilworth dies. He was "the dean of local shoe repair shop owners" in Savannah. St. Louis Pender, the well known barber, dies.

1956 — Segregation signs removed from Union Station. However, in the 1950's white Savannah generally accepts segregation as the normal arrangement of society. Milton Hall, one of the first black policemen dies. The Rev. Ralph Mark Gilbert dies. He was the father of the modern civil rights movement in Savannah. Dr. F. Belcher dies. He practiced medicine in Savannah for fifty-three years. The Falcons Club is organized in the basement of Dr. Henry M. Collier's home.

1957 — The Chatham County Christian Ministerial Association protests ban on blacks at Tybee beach. Nurse Ella May Stevens Sams, a 1906 graduate of the Georgia Infirmary, receives a bowl for her more than fifty years in the nursing profession. She was one of the first public health nurses in Savannah. Madam Birdie Freeman dies. She opened her beauty parlor in 1914 and used the Poro system of hair care.

1958 — The Hub petitions the city and county to appoint blacks to the Board of Education. The Board renames the Powell Laboratory School in Thunderbolt as the Sol C. Johnson School. Mrs. Mamie K. Singleton of 526 Duffy Street is first black chosen to serve as foreman of a Chatham County Superior Court jury. The Board of Education changes the name of the Springfield Terrace School to Pearl Lee Smith School. Mrs. Charlotte S. Curley dies. She was the superintendent of Mills Memorial Home for twenty-five years. Augustus Hayes dies. He operated Gus' Lounge on old Augusta Road and was a prominent businessman for about twenty-two years.

1959 — Blacks attempt to integrate the Municipal Golf Course and begin to move into all white neighborhoods. Blacks' request to use the public library is denied. Eleven blacks fail in their attempt to play at the Municipal Golf Course. Reputed "numbers king" William (Sloppy Joe) Bellinger, dies. About 10,000 persons attend his funeral in the Flamingo Club on West Gwinnett Street extension. James H. Butler, associate editor of the *Savannah Tribune* since 1910, dies. Savannah born Dr. Milton D. Bryant dies. He was trained at Meharry Medical College and practiced in Savannh for thirty-five years.

1960 — Eleven blacks arrested for holding a "wade-in" at Tybee beach. Five blacks are arrested for refusing to leave lunch counter at Levy's Department store on Broughton Street. The branch stages demonstrations at S. H. Kress, Livingston's Pharmacy and other places of business. Three blacks are arrested during a "sit-down" in white restaurants. The Mayor appoints a bi-racial committee to consider racial problems. The NAACP disapproves of this committee. Twenty-three blacks headed by NAACP officials try to use Savannah parks and recreation facilities. Sixteen blacks hold "kneel-in" at five white downtown churches. The *Savannah Tribune* regards Hosea Williams' crusade for voters as a "giant step on the road to complete equality and freedom for the Negro in Chatham

County." The Rev. Curtis Jackson, Moses L. Williams, Revs. Patterson, Stell, Curtis Cooper, and Mrs. Mercedes Wright, address protestors. Blacks are thirty-five and a half percent of the city's population. City Council passes ordinance to control Negro picketing of white merchants. Blacks seek integration of the public library. Eleven blacks who tried to use Tybee beach arrested for having changed to bathing suits in their vehicles. Holy Apostles Episcopal Church welcomes Negroes attending their service. Sit-ins continue at lunch counters. Mayor Mingledorf resigns in face of integration's demands.

1961 — Mayor Malcolm McLean ends segregation at the public libraries. Clifford Hardwick becomes the first black supervisor at the Board of Education. An eighteen-month boycott of Broughton Street begins at Morrison's Cafeteria, Kress and Azalea Room at Levy's Department Store, and others. The Georgia Court of Appeals upholds the conviction of thirty-two black "sit-ins." Corporal A. Owens, a Paris Island marine, is denied admission to Armstrong College. Lunch counters are integrated. Savannah Transit buses integrated. About twenty-one black students protest the dismissal of Principal A. F. Cheatham of Sol Johnson School. Beach and Tompkins threaten to join the protest. Blacks end boycott of downtown stores. The city of Savannah opens its municipal golf links to Negroes. Council is discussing a petition by blacks to desegregate all municipal parks. Walter S. Scott dies. He opened his first business in 1903. Louis B. Toomer dies. He was born in Savannah in 1897, and started Carver State Bank in 1927. Dr. Henry M. Collier dies. He graduated from Meharry Medical College in 1913, and headed the X-Ray departmernt of Charity Hospital. He was named doctor of the year in 1958. Juanita Williams runs unsuccessfully for clerk of Superior Court. The Rev. Ralph Mark Gilbert establishes the first Georgia State Conferternce of the NAACP. He is elected the president.

1962 — The Rev. S. Scott Stell, and thirty-five others, file *Stell v. Board of Education* (Civil Action No. 1316) against the Board of Education seeking integrated schooling. Seventeen white parents file suit to prevent the integration of the schools. The NAACP petitions for the appointment of blacks to the Board of Education. Many black residents in Troup ward displaced by whites. The branch also boycotts Derst Baking Company. Mrs. Henry Wilson Hodge dies. This white woman was unique in that she donated very liberally to black causes over many years. She contributed to the Mills Memorial Home, Hodge Memorial Kindergarten and Day Nursery, Savannah State College, Frank Callen Boys Club and Charity Hospital and Training School for Nurses. The Board of Education named a school on Victory Drive in her honor.

1963 — The U. S. Supreme Court overturns the conviction of six blacks who attempted to use the Daffin Park playground. First black students register at Armstrong College. Mayor MacLean meets with black leaders in an attempt to stop demonstrations. U.S. District Judge F. M. Scarlett issues final judgment in the school desegregation case. The Rev. Ralph Abernathy addresses a large rally. Hosea Williams arrested. City Council banns racial marches. Black students apply to transfer to Savannah High School and six apply to Groves. Chatham County Crusade for Voters is accused of being communist inspired. Otis Johnson, first Negro student at Armstrong State College, is on the dean's list. The Rev. O. E. Cleveland pastor of St. John's Baptist Church dies. He added some 2,000 members to the congregation.

1964 — Congress passes the Civil Rights Act. Racially offensive signs are removed from Memorial Medical Center. These signs have already been removed from City Hall, the Court House, health department and other public places in the city. The Poll tax is abolished. Mrs. Esther F. Garrison is first black woman appointed to the Board of Education. Lawrence D. Perry is the first black male appointed to Board of Education. Charity Hospital closes. The Rev. P. A. Patterson runs for County Commissioner, Sam Williams for sheriff and attorney Bobby C. Mayfield for the State Senate. They are all unsuccessful.

Blacks petition for the integration of Daffin Park swimming pool. Fifty black junior and senior high school pupils transferred to Savannah and Groves high schools. The Board of Education approves a plan to speed integration of schools. Otis Johnson is first black graduate of Armstrong State College. Sundial honoring Louis B. Toomer installed in Chatham Square. The Rev. L. Scott Stell becomes the first black appointed to the Transit Authority.

1965 —Black youths attempt a "kneel-in" at four downtown white churches and are turned away. State policy of school segregation officially ends.

1966 —U.S. District Judge F. M. Scarlet signs order calling for the placing of all students according to their mental abilities regardless of race. Some 20,000 black students now occupy classrooms formerly used by whites. About 205 black teachers teach white pupils and 289 white teachers teach black students. Mrs. Ursuline Ingersoll appointed supervisor of library services at the Board of Education.

1967 —The local NAACP chapter sponsors a series of lectures by Professor Robert W. Gadsden on the black experience in Savannah. Westley W. Law and ten members of the NAACP appear before the Library Board in connection with books on blacks and integration. The NAACP accuses the police department of brutality.

1968 —Bobby Hill is the first black elected to the Georgia Legislature from Chatham County in one hundred years. The Rev. L. Scott Stell, pastor of Bethlehem Baptist Church, is the first black elected a County Commissioner. Westley W. Law President of the local NAACP complains about the injustice suffered by blacks in housing, education and employment. Three youth leaders of the NAACP present Mayor Curtis Lewis a petition requesting 674 summer jobs. The mayor finds the petition "disturbing and disconcerting."

1969 —W. W. Law declares rights of blacks an empty sham due to lack of economic opportunity. Attorney Mayfield endorsed for First District Congressional seat.

1970 — Bowles C. Ford becomes the first black ever elected City Alderman. Ford presides over council meeting as the mayor and the mayor pro tem, are absent. The Catholic Church plans to close

St. Pius High School. Savannah Lions Club opposes busing as a means to foster integration. Attorney Bobby Hill asks U.S. Circuit Court to reject the school board's integration plan. E. Mathis considers run for mayor of Savannah or as city alderman. Black business and professional group organized. Blacks request black history to be taught in public schools. Blacks are almost fifty percent of city's population. The Rev. James M. Floyd, who carried the Savannah branch's banner during the march on Washington in 1963, is shot in the NAACP office at 1214 West Broad Street.

1971 — The District Court orders schools desegregated and about 10,000 whites leave the system. Westley W. Law complains that Mills Lane and the Historic Savannah have "kept us out of most of that river front area." He calls for a shake up in the housing law.

1972 – James C. Carthon protests the Savannah Housing Authority's intention to spend millions of dollars on the riverfront renewal project rather than on improving housing projects in black areas.

1973 – John White and twenty-seven black officers file a class-action suit against the discriminatory policies of the city in the hiring and promotion black officers.

1974 – Westley W. Law turned away from Bull Street Baptist Church. The local NAACP unveils tablet honoring former chapter president the Rev. Ralph Mark Gilbert. The chapter accuses the local radio and television stations of practicing racial discrimination in hiring.

1975 – Westley W. Law sponsors a Black Heritage Downtown Walking Tour to emphasize the contribution of blacks to Savannah's development.

1976 – Westley W. Law resigns as president of the local NAACP and Curtis V. Cooper succeeds him. Law organizes the Yamacraw branch of the Study of Afro-American Life and History and starts the Negro Heritage Trail.

1979 —Governor George Busbee appoints attorney Eugene Gadsden to Superior Court of Chatham County. He is the first black to hold that position. W. W. Law's Savannah Negro Heritage Trail from Colonial Days to Emancipation gets national press exposure and international renown on the Voice of America shortwave broadcast. Prof. Robert W. Gadsden dies. He taught school for forty-five years. Lawrence D. Perry dies.

1980 – The local NAACP chapter urges the firing of a teacher who struck a student at Hesse Elementary School. The chapter opposes the School Board's redistricting plan. Esther F. Garrison runs against Curtis Cooper for the presidency of the local chapter. Cooper is reelected. City Council names a Cloverdale park in honor of Boles Ford. Dr. Phillip Cooper dies. He practiced dentistry for some thirty years. Father Gustave Caution dies. He was rector of St. Stephen's Episcopal Church from 1931 to 1938 and the rector of St. Matthew's for twenty-two years. John Sanders Delaware dies. He was born in the Old Fort, around Greene Square, and after attending East Broad Street School graduated from the Georgia State College for Colored Youth, now Savannah State University, in 1915. He was superintendent of the Sunday School at First African Baptist Church for sixty years and chairman of the Deacon Board for twenty-five years. Delaware served as secretary of the local branch of the NAACP and was scout master of Troop 48 and chairman of the Negro Division of the Boy Scouts. He earned scouting's highest honor, the silver Beaver award. He also served on many boards and organizations, especially the Frank Callen Boys' Club. He somehow also found time to function as a mailman for forty-five years. On his death, Westley W. Law ascribed to him the Negro saying: "Every shut eye ain' sleep and every goodbye ain' gone."

1981 – NAACP president Curtis V. Cooper complains that Reagan cutbacks hurt the poor. Blacks protest concert by South African boys choir. NAACP sponsors first Freedom Fund Dinner. Former Mayor Malcolm MacLean and Mrs. Lottie Bell Banner are honorees. Dr. Stephen McDew, Jr., dies. He practiced here for forty years.

1982 — NAACP opposes city and county consolidation. Blacks oppose the establishment of a prison camp near a black neighborhood. Madam Carrie Cargo dies. She was a leader in beauty culture in Savannah. She operated the Cargo Beauty School and Shop for many years.

1983 — Newly formed Southern Leadership Council chapter seeks an investigation of Sheriff Carl Griffin and protest discriminatory hiring by local businesses. Floyd Adams, Sr., "Press Boy," dies. He was a co-founder of the *Savannah Herald*.

1984 — Dollar days demonstrate black economic influence. Black leaders discuss crime and teen pregnancy. The local NAACP stages a counter K.K.K. rally. The Rev. Scott Stell and Leopold Adler honored at NAACP Freedom Fund Dinner. The Rev. Edgar Quarterman dies. He pastored the Second African Baptist Church from 1949 to 1983. He started the boy scouts at Second African Baptist Church and was the first black appointed to the Park and Tree Commission.

1985 — Monument to Bishop Henry McNeal Turner is dedicated. The NAACP denounces the new Board of Education school plan. The Rev. L. Scott Stell dies. He pastored Bethlehem Baptist Church for thirty-three years. Walter Bogan, Sr., dies. He worked at the *Savannah Morning News* for more than forty years.

1986 – Martin L. King, Jr., parade celebrated. Blacks protest shooting of Otis Parker. The NAACP accepts school board's plan.

1987 – The Board of Education adopts magnet programs in some schools.

1988 – Dr. Albert Lafayette dies. He was born in Savannah and practiced dentistry for more than sixty years.

1989 — Mail bomb kills Fifth District City Alderman and NAACP Attorney Robbie Robinson. He was one of the first blacks to graduate from Savannah High School and later graduated from the University of Georgia Law School. Dr. Henry M. Collier, Jr., dies. This family gave over 160 years to the medical and dental care of blacks in Savannah.

1990 — West Broad Street is changed to Martin L. King Jr., Boulevard. Some blacks wanted Thirty-Seventh Street to get the honor.

1991 — Clarence Thomas is appointed to the U. S. Supreme Court.

1992 – Floyd Adams Jr., is named mayor pro tem. Captain Sam Stevens dies. He operated excursion boats on the Savannah River for many years.

1993 – The Board of Education petitions the District Court for unitary status. Boles C. Ford dies. He was the first black ever elected to City Council.

1994 —The Federal Court ends the 1962 desegregation case. The Rev. John Q. Adams dies. He was the pastor of Mount Zion Baptist Church for fifty-nine years and taught at Beach for over forty years. He graduated from Morehouse College in Atlanta in 1917.

1995 — Floyd Adams, Jr., is elected first African American mayor of Savannah.

1996 – Coach Joe Greene dies. He was a teacher, coach and administrator, at Beach for more than thirty years. The Ralph Mark Gilbert Civil Rights Museum opens in the former Wage Earners Bank building.

1998 — Dr. J. W. Jamerson dies. He practiced dentistry for fifty-five years. The present Dr. J. W. Jamerson, his father and grandfather before him, have together practiced dentistry in Savannah for 124 years. From 1905 to the present there has always been a black dentist, named Dr. J. W. Jamerson in Savannah.

1999 — City Council has a black majority for the first time.

2000 — Bobby Hill dies. He was the first black elected to the Georgia house since James Porter and James Simms were elected during Reconstruction. Curtis V. Cooper dies. He was president of the NAACP local chapter from 1976 to his death. Cooper served as director of the Westside Urban

Center for more than tweny years and was chairman of the Deacon Board at Second African Baptist Church. Judge Eugene Gadsden dies. He was the first black to serve as a judge of the Superior Court in Chatham County. African Americans are sixty-two percent of the population.

2002 — Westley W. Law dies. He led the NAACP during the tumultuous years of the 1960s and left his mark on the city. He was a preservationist of the first rank and helped to organize the King- Tisdell Foundation and the Ralph Mark Gilbert Civil Rights Museum in 1996. Frank Bynes dies. He was a "keeper of the story" of black life in Savannah.

Index

African American Monument, 17, 48, 49
Bay Street, 17, 49
Father Andrew Bryan, 20, 60
Beach Institute Neighborhood, 17, 52, 53, 54, 55
Bethlehem Missionary Baptist Church, 17, 21, 23, 59
Bronze Mayor, 32
Broughton Street, 17
Frank Callen Boys & Girls Club, 54
The Rev. William Campbell, 45
Madam Carrie Cargo, 42, 97
Carver State Bank, 33, 34
The Drs. Collier, 42, 85, 87
Cotton Exchange, 49
Custom House, 49
Curry Town, 17, 19
Cuyler/Brownville, 17, 22-29
Cuyler Street School, 23, 25
Col. John H. Deveaux, 48, 67, 70
Catherine & Jane Deveaux's Underground School, 17
Discovering Black Savannah, 17, 18, 19
Dunbar Theater, 39, 40, 90
Entertainment, 38, 39, 40
First African Baptist Church, 17, 43-46
First Black Public School, 17, 53-55
First Bryan Baptist Church, 17, 59, 60
Madam Birdie Freeman, 41, 42
Florence Street School, 26, 27
Frog Town, 17, 19
Robert W. Gadsden School, 19, 21
Ralph Mark Gilbert Civil Rights Museum, 17, 33, 106
Bishop Emanuel Grace, 27, 28
Hair Styling, 41
The Drs. Jamerson, 42, 43, 89
Gus Hayes, 39
Josephine Stiles Jennings, 40
Charlie Johnson, 41
Sol C. Johnson, 40, 41, 68-70
Martin L. King Jr., Boulevard, 17, 29-43

King-Tisdell Cottage, 17, 54, 55
Laurel Grove Cemetery South, 17, 28, 29
The Rev. George Liele, 20, 21
St. Matthew's Episcopal Church, 17, 24, 25, 55
Mills Memorial Home, 27
Most Pure Heart of Mary, 26
McKane/Charity Hospital, 24, 25, 26
William McKelvey, 43
The Drs. McDew, 43, 88
Andrew Monroe, 37, 91
Captain John Newton, 48
Old Fort, 56
Palen United Methodist, 28
Pekin Theatre, 40
Royall Funeral Home, 35, 36, 37
St. Philip's Monumental African Methodist Episcopal Church, 17, 59, 61
Savannah Visitor Center, 17, 19
Savannah Savings Bank, 33
Savannah Pharmacy, 34
Savannah River/Street, 17, 47
Second African Baptist Church, 17, 50, 51, 53
Slave sales, 12
Captain John Newton, 48
Captain Edward Seabrook, 37, 39
Captain Hermon Sengstake, 48
Captain John Starr, 48
Star Theater, 40
Steele Funeral Home, 37, 71
The Drs. Tyson, 43, 86
The Unitarian Church (St. Stephen's Episcopal), 17, 53-55
Wage Earners Bank, 32, 33
West Broad Street School, 56
Madam Ruth Williams, 42
Connie Wimberly, 39, 93
Yamacraw, 17, 56-61